Charles Rampini

Letters from Jamaica

The Land of Streams and Woods

Charles Rampini

Letters from Jamaica
The Land of Streams and Woods

ISBN/EAN: 9783743408401

Manufactured in Europe, USA, Canada, Australia, Japa

Cover: Foto ©ninafisch / pixelio.de

Manufactured and distributed by brebook publishing software (www.brebook.com)

.

Charles Rampini

Letters from Jamaica

CONTENTS.

I.

IN KINGSTON HARBOUR.

"WELL, I'm blessed!" said the man at the wheel;
"them cussed niggers once more!" "Running up
into the harbour, sir!" echoed the steward with a
face suggestive of coming fees; "and them black
fellows in plenty awaitin' for you on the wharf."
There they were certainly—woolly heads, bare feet,
ebon faces, loud voices—all ready and waiting this fine
February morning, though the sun was hardly up, to
pounce upon us and our baggage, as we left what
had been our floating home for the last three weeks.
Eighteen days out, and prosperous winds almost all
the way. And now, in the clear bright light of a
tropical morning, we were at last in sight of the
"Land of Streams."

Of course, we had had our own share of "incidents"
to vary the weary monotony of the voyage. Our
engines had gone wrong on one occasion, as they were
in duty bound to do, and we had been delayed
twenty-four hours in consequence. For three whole
days, too, we experienced rather dirty weather;
strong winds though fair, and heavy seas, which
made us all very uncomfortable and not a little cross.

Life on board ship becomes rather a burden when
the saloon is dark as pitch, the skylights battened
down, candles burning at meal times, and the
"fiddles" on the tables. Our meals then cease to
be the bright oases in the flat level of our existence which at other times they are felt to be.
Accidents are too frequent to be pleasant. I have a
pretty strong recollection of one evil day in particular,
when I received at breakfast the contents of the
lamp—nasty, green, rancid, evil-smelling oil—over
my plate and hands, and at lunch had the felicity of
feeling a glass of port wine gently insinuating itself
into my sleeve, "and so on upwards," until its trickling course was arrested at a point considerably past
my elbow. But, in return for these discomforts, we
had the chance of seeing "sea scenery" such as we
never had witnessed before. The eye never tired of
watching the solid masses of water, the rippling
clouds of spray, the breaking, white-tipped curling
waves. Then the varying lights and colours of the
billows—grey, green, and blue at times, and sometimes in the evening, with the flush of sunset upon
them, a delicate purple, or rather a tint between
purple and magenta, which is not to be expressed in
words. It was a noble consolation, even though our
cabins were soaking with water. Then by degrees,
as we got into warmer latitudes, we came upon shoals
of flying fish, and one solitary specimen we caught.
Next our cow took ill, and one sad eve was gathered
to its fathers; and a mysterious malady which was
not sea-sickness attacked our travelling poultry-yard.

But now all our troubles were over—we had arrived. These cocoa-nut trees, and these white rocks, these crumpled mountains, and this gently-curving bay, was "that wondrous isle in the western seas" which we had come five thousand miles to explore. And truly our first view of the island, seen from the deck of the steamer as we steamed slowly past the long coral reef called the Palisades which guards the entrance to the harbour, in no degree belied our expectations. Not that Kingston itself, as it stretched along the shore with its dingy wharves and its low-lying dilapidated wooden houses, added much to the beauty of the landscape. But behind and above rose the magnificent range of the Blue Mountains, clothed, up to their very summits, with verdure, their green sides furrowed into many a fissure and gully by the impetuous rains which in spring and autumn sweep down the mountain sides and find their way to the sea in innumerable rivers and torrents. Dotted amongst them nestled many a white house and villa, for here "in the hills," to use a Creoleism, is the favourite abode of the better class of Jamaica society, whilst at a giddy height above these, on the very crest of the hill, and apparently amongst the clouds, stood the military station of Newcastle, nearly 4000 feet above the sea—its snowy tents and houses stretching away over the rocks, like a flock of sheep on a Highland mountain. We had but time to take a general view of the scene, when we were made fast to our moorings at the Company's wharf.

In one moment, like the sudden apparition of a

B

troupe of demons in a pantomime, the ship was full
of negroes.   Swarming like ants, they penetrated
into every hole and corner of the vessel.   You found
them in your cabin ; you found them in the saloon.
One caught up your portmanteau, and another your
dressing-case.   Grinning, laughing, shouting, quarrel-
ling, the perspiration pouring off their sable faces,
they strove and fought and squabbled over our trunks
and packages.   Before I knew where I was, my
cherished travelling bag had disappeared over the
gangway; and I record with pleasure my obligations
to that most excellent of men, my bedroom steward,
for rescuing myself and the remainder of my property from the clutches of the rapacious crew.   One
by one our little travelling society began to disperse,
each on his or her different course of life.   There
was the little Cuban lady with her short dress and
her high heeled boots, and her chattering not unmusical voice.   There was the pair of Spaniards who sat
opposite to us at dinner and devoured the dessert
before their neighbours had finished their soup.
There was the sullen passenger whom, it was re-
ported, our good captain, for sundry high crimes and
misdemeanours, had threatened to put in irons.
There was that long, lank, sallow Brazilian, who
seemed "to carry some great sorrow next his heart,"
which he could only assuage by eating prodigious
quantities of cheese and marmalade at breakfast-time.
There was the fat English lady with her Skye terrier,
her patent washing machine, and her pots of drooping fuchsias and geraniums.   There was the Mora-

vian "brother" and his lot-selected helpmate; and
the two planters, evidently "born near the plantain
root," who thought Jamaica was going to the devil;
and the country shopkeeper—he called himself a
merchant and wrote J.P. after his name in the address
we presented to the captain; and lastly there were
our noble selves, with whom we trust the reader will
in due time become better acquainted.

Scarcely had the last passenger left the ship when
began that most useful but most disagreeable of pro-
cesses—the coaling of the steamer. This service,
which is entirely performed by negroes, is said to cost
the Company, at Kingston-alone, no less than £2000
a year. One after another in a long line, men and
women, black as the coals they carried, chanting a
wild recitative, and walking with that peculiar swing
which is characteristic of the black race all over the
world, they trooped up the gangway to empty their
baskets in the hold. These "coal boys," and still
more so the "coal girls," are a peculiar class. Lazy,
idle, dissolute, they do nothing between the departure of one ship and the arrival of another but loaf
round the gates of the Company's wharf, or under
the piazzas of the houses in the neighbouring streets,
eating oranges and abusing each other in the most
obscene of language.

We had the fortune to witness a fight between
two of these interesting maidens. Catching her
opponent by the neck, vixen No. 1 commenced the
attack by delivering a vigorous "buck" with her
head right in front of her antagonist—a compliment

which was instantly returned. Now both were wrestling on the ground, legs twined with legs, and arms with arms, and the blood flowing pretty freely on either side. How long this might have lasted we cannot say, for nobody seemed to think it his duty to interfere. But just at this juncture a constable was seen approaching, and the two termagants bleeding, wounded, almost naked, hurling abuse at each other all the time, with many tears and many objurgations, were incontinently marched off to "the cage."

Our first business on leaving the ship was to provide ourselves with lodgings. So hailing a "'bus," as the Kingston cabs are called, we started to seek the hotel to which we had been recommended. This "'bus" of ours was certainly a most curious and rudimentary structure. It was, in fact, nothing more than a seat on wheels with poles attached to each corner, over which a shabby piece of tarpaulin was stretched by way of protection from the sun. Our driver was an impish-looking boy, apparently about fifteen, with a scarlet sash tied round his waist, and a roll of white cotton festooned with blue calico twisted round his somewhat indefinable head-gear. He smoked incessantly, all the time viciously tugging the ropes which served him for reins, and almost sawing open the mouth of his miserable horse, which, with bones projecting through its skin, and a weary beseeching look in its lustreless eyes, was doing its best to drag the over-laden vehicle through the unpaved streets. Like almost all its fellows our 'bus had its name—" The Lukkey "—(Query, *lucky ?*) conspicuously painted on its back. Some of these names were very amusing. On our short journey up East Street we passed " The Pride of the East," " The People's Favourite," with a rather handsome coloured girl seated in it; " It shines for all," " The Army and Navy," " Something must be done," " Self-help," and " The Good Time Coming."

In due time, and after a prodigious amount of tumbling and jolting, we were landed at the door of a large and desolate-looking building, which the driver informed us was the " Hall " (for by this grand name are inns known in Jamaica) to which we were bound. We entered upon a court-yard paved with brick, around which half-a-dozen men and women were idly sitting. Two wall-eyed horses were being rubbed down; sable damsels seated on the ground were wash- ing ewers and basins and towels. A rug was being shaken from a balcony overhead. A couple of tur- keys, three enraged Guinea fowls, some poultry, two goats, and a lean dog were wandering about at their own sweet wills; and the filthy condition of the courtyard justified the presumption that this litter had not been removed for a week. As we were wonderingly looking around to see whether we had not made a mistake and entered the " curtilage " of a private dwelling-house, one of the women, whom we afterwards discovered to be the proprietrix of the establishment, without rising from her chair, wished us an indolent and indifferent " good morning." We were about to commence an apology for our intrusion, when she suddenly interrupted us by calling to a dirty black boy who was passing, "Thomas, show the gentlemen into the hall, and tell the house-woman to put water into No. 24." Then, without taking further notice of us, she turned to her next neighbour and commenced a tirade upon the " *vileness* " of servants in Jamaica, and of her own in particular. Following our guide up-stairs we were ushered into a large room, where an old negress, on her knees, smoking the stump of a cigar with the lighted end in her mouth, was cleaning the polished floor. Off this central apartment the bedrooms diverged in all directions. Into one of these we were inducted by the sulky boy. The room was gloomy as a vault. A bed, a chair, and a basin-stand constituted all the furniture. A little strip of matting by our bedside was all our carpet. There were few traces of that West Indian luxury of which we had heard so much before leaving home. Breakfast was served to us in a broad verandah overlooking the street. We had oysters from the mangrove trees at Port Royal, a brilliant scarlet " snapper," an excellent fish, but, like all tropical fishes, soft and flabby in substance ; brain fritters, a small biscuit called "crackers" soaked in butter, stuffed " garden eggs," a most delicious vegetable, roasted plantains, a piled-up plate of golden oranges and a pine-apple. Our drink was iced water, but tea and coffee were to be had for the asking. Such was our first meal in Jamaica.

II.

IN KINGSTON STREETS.

KINGSTON has all the characteristics of a town which has lost its self-respect. Like a man who has seen better days, it has given up attending even to its personal appearance. "It looks what it is," said Sewell, who visited it in 1860—"a place where money has been made, but can be made no more. It is used up, and cast aside as useless."[1] Broken walls, charred beams, crumbling ruins meet one in all directions. Harbour Street, the main thoroughfare, is unpaved; and gutters to carry off the heavy rains which fall at certain seasons of the year are unknown. At such times the streets are rivers; business is suspended; many of the stores do not take down their shutters, and the miserable town looks more miserable than ever.

It would be difficult to imagine a place whose general aspect depresses one so much as Kingston. The town rises gradually from the sea to the height of about 100 feet. It reaches its highest elevation at the racecourse, and its lowest at the Company's wharf. Between the two, and right in the middle

[1] *Ordeal of Free Labour in the British West Indies*, p. 175. New York. 1861.

of the city, is the Parade; an open square presently being laid out by Government as a garden, with a waterless fountain in the midst, and a statue of Lord Metcalfe. Facing each other, top and bottom, are the Theatre and the Parish Church. The other two sides of the square are occupied by the old barracks (soon to be converted into a handsome court-house), and a church built of red brick, belonging, we believe, to the Wesleyan denomination.

Owing to the unmodulated flatness of its site, Kingston, from the water, presents the appearance of a mere confused mass of sun-baked buildings. Close to the sea, truly, stands a large circular iron building recently erected by the Government as a metropolitan market; but here, as was right and proper in a case where public money was to be expended, convenience has been studied in preference to beauty; and the structure, though handsome enough of its kind, can hardly be said to add much to the amenity of the landscape. The only other architectural feature which breaks the dull monotony of the sky-line is what looks like a little white pigeon-cot hidden away at the back of the town. This is the spire of the Parish Church, and the only attempt at a spire in Kingston; and doubtless the good people of the town would be very proud of it, were it not that the Spanishtonians, between whom and the Kingstonians there exists a feeling of jealousy, not to say a feud, possess one attached to their cathedral exactly of the same shape and size, and situated in very nearly the same position in their midst.

There is a marvellous lack of appreciation of the beautiful in the Creole mind.[1] Tropical towns are generally little more than a group of barns and sheds. The public buildings are pre-eminently the former : the private buildings are too often little better than the latter. This is the more remarkable, because the sites of these towns, especially when they date back, as many of them do, to the old Spanish days, have been selected with a wonderful eye to their natural surroundings—at the head of land-locked bays, perched on rocky crags, or commanding some wide and spreading view of strath or sea, of bold and escarped mountain, or green and cane-covered plain.

In Kingston, the streets, although laid out on the most formal and geometrical principles, are clumsy and irregular. The houses, with their steep, shingled roofs, are of all sorts and sizes. They cannot even boast " a picturesque confusion." Most of them are fronted with covered verandahs called " piazzas," provided with jalousies to fend off the vertical sun, which gives them the cheerful look of houses shut up for the season, whilst the family are out of town. The principal entrance is as often on the second storey as on the first, and at the side of the house rather than in the front. The ordinary arrangement of a Jamaica house is something like this : Entering

[1] The word Creole, in its literal acceptation, simply means a person born in the West Indies, independent of all complexional distinctions. In England " it is most commonly used to express a mulatto ; " but it is a mistake to suppose, as *The Saturday Review* in an article on Creole Grammar (March 26, 1870) lays it down, that " its strict meaning is a native of a colony, of European race, as opposed to an immigrant."

upon the piazza, which is fitted up with rocking
chairs and ottomans, you pass to the drawing-room,
off which the bedrooms diverge on every side.   The
dining-room is generally upon the ground floor, and to
reach this you have either to descend by a trap stair
or by the same outside staircase by which you gained
admission to the drawing-room.   The bedrooms,
especially in country houses, are small and ill ven-
tilated.   In " old time " houses the only room of
anything like decent dimensions is the dining-room
—a striking instance of the social habits of the
colony in its so-called palmy days.

There are no public buildings worthy of the name
in Kingston as yet.   The churches, except in one or
two instances, are without the slightest claims to
architectural beauty.   The Parish Church is remark- ·
able only from its old mahogany altar-screen, and the
antiquity of some of its monuments.   Close before
the altar-rails lie the remains of the gallant Admiral
Benbow ; and the old song still commemorates

> " How the people thronged very much
> To see brave Admiral Benbow laid in Kingston town church."

The Church of England has never been the church
of the colony ; consequently the number of Dissenting chapels, both in Kingston and throughout the
island, far exceeds those belonging to the (Dis-)
Establishment.   The Baptists, Jews, Wesleyans,
Methodists, the Established and Free Churches
of Scotland, Moravians, Roman Catholics, and In-
dependents, all have numerous places of worship of
their own.

Of the public establishments of the colony, the best conducted are the General Penitentiary, the Lunatic Asylum, and the Public Hospital. The ruling principle of the two former is the utilisation of the labour of the inmates. In the former brick and tile making, coir and oakum picking, boat building, printing, and lime burning are successfully carried on. In the country districts the convicts in the local prisons are employed in road making, pasture cleaning, and other agricultural works. In Kingston the streets are cleaned and kept in repair by their labour. In the General Penitentiary the treadmill is used to grind corn. The female prisoners, who are brought into the prison under masks as hideous as those of a San Benito, do all the washing of the establishment, and also the ships' washing for the steamers of the Royal Mail Company. Up to a very recent period, the hair of all women undergoing punishment with hard labour, in the Penitentiary, was cut off on their entering the establishment, and, as at home, no part of their punishment was felt more. We have been told by an official connected with the prison establishment in the colony, that it was a common practice for a woman who felt herself pretty sure of being convicted, to cut off her wool before her trial, and give it to a friend to keep for her until her term of "labour at the Penn," as the negroes jocularly call it, was over. On coming out, it could easily be tacked on again to her head by the help of a needle and thread. Her thick bandana handkerchief would, of course, conceal all traces of the operation. Within the last year, however, the cropping of female convicts' hair has been abolished by the Governor.

Deserters from the road gangs are punished with iron collars fastened round their necks. Women endure solitary confinement in a detached turret called the punishment tower. The negro prisoners have the thick iron doors of their cells closed during both the day and the night; the white prisoners, on the other hand, are confined behind an iron grating, which admits both air and light.

To the negro imprisonment is no disgrace, and even with hard labour very little punishment. During his incarceration he lives in clover. He is fed much better than he is at home. His clothes, albeit they are more like rice-sacks than anything else, are sufficient for his wants. The actual deprivation of freedom is a sentimental luxury with which he can readily dispense.

He returns to his country district, on the expiration of his sentence, a made-man in the estimation of all his neighbours. We remember a case where a man, on coming out of prison, after undergoing a long sentence of penal servitude, was met by his friends at the entrance of his native village, mounted on horseback, and in this gallant style conducted to his home, where a feast awaited him. A " dance " and its accompaniments concluded the " demonstration " of that eventful day.

It is a decided misfortune to the traveller arriving in Jamaica to be landed in the early morning,

as was our miserable lot. Breakfast was over by
nine o'clock; and there was the day before us; and
in this country "in the day no man can work." But
we could not rest in the house. So mounting " pug-
rees " and white umbrellas, we sallied forth immediately after breakfast to make acquaintance with the
Kingston streets. By this time all the town was
alive, and Harbour Street was crowded. Clerks and
shopmen were hurrying to their respective offices
and stores, some on foot, some in 'buses, and not a
few in buggies.. Handsome equipages were dashing
past: this, with a merchant on his way to his count-
ing-house; that, with a party of ladies going shop-
ping before the heat became intense. Higglers of all
descriptions were vigorously plying their trade.
Coolies with baskets of vegetables on their heads;
girls with cedar-boxes full of sugar cakes of every
kind; boys with bundles of walking-sticks; vendors
of tripe and " chickling ;" men with trays of king-
fish. At the corners of the streets, with little boxes
by their sides, women were selling pins and tapes
and braids. There stood one with a basket of parched
maize on her head; here another tempted you with
a heap of rosy apples which the ice-ship had just
brought over from America; a third offered you a
little saucerful of Alpine strawberries, brought down
that morning from the Newcastle hills; whilst another
exposed some magnificent artichokes, which had also
been grown amongst the mountains. Each had his
or her *spécialité*. Nobody had more than one kind
of article to sell. He who sold booby eggs had

nothing to do with the vendor of eggs of ordinary poultry. The dealer in radishes sold neither carrots nor turnips. If you wanted fruit, you had to buy your bananas from one person, your oranges from a second, and your pine-apples from a third. It was impossible to avoid the feeling that we were in a foreign city, and surrounded by a foreign population. These people spoke English, it is true; but English which we had the greatest difficulty to understand. The tones and inflections of their voices, the indolent " yawny-drawly " way, to use Coleridge's phrase, in which every word was pronounced, the shrill pitch of their sentences, were not English, whatever the words might have been. Then, too, the streets were filled with men of all nationalities, and of every shade of colour. There were yellow Chinamen, lanky Americans, fat and comfortable-looking Jews, lively midshipmen from the men-of-war at Port Royal, coolies from Madras, and Scotchmen from Aberdeen. We met several parties of Cuban ladies, with mantillas over their heads, and several Haïtiens were pointed out, whom recent events had driven away from their own country. Of beggars we saw very few, and these were chiefly lepers. Begging does not seem to pay in this country. One wretched creature, suffering from that particular form of the disease which goes by the African name of " coco-bay," asked us for an alms. His hands and feet were toeless and fingerless masses, and his arm had withered up almost to his elbow. It is one of the disgraces of Jamaica that such loathsome objects

should be allowed to go at large. The street cries
were neither very musical nor very amusing. They
seemed all to be uttered in a whining, nasal, dis-
contented tone, and at the shrillest possible pitch.
" Ripe mangoes gwine (going) past ! " was more like
a complaint than an invitation to purchase. " Coffee,
sixpence a quart ! " might have been a wail of anguish,
for aught we knew to the contrary. " Starch ! " was a
most unmistakeable scream, and " Fresh oysters gwine
past ! " more like an Irish " croon " than anything
we had heard in our lives. At the door of one of the
large haberdashery stores, we overheard a funny conversation between two fashionably-dressed coloured
girls, which amusingly illustrates their fondness for
over-adornment in all things, even in their language.
" Marning, ma'am ! " said Jane to Justina, eyeing her
from head to foot, and doubtless admiring with just
the faintest suspicion of envy her brilliant bandana
and her long flowing skirts, her gaudy rings, and
drooping earrings. " Marning, ma'am ! how you feel
yourself to-day ? " " Pretty so-so, I tank you."
"Quite warm to-day," continued the other, fanning
herself. " Yes, ma'am," was the reply ; " indeed, the
heatment is very greatment ! " " Yes, ma'am ! " And
making each other a low curtsey, the two friends
parted. The " heatment " had indeed grown un-
pleasantly " greatment," and the glare from the
broiling streets was making us nearly blind. With
soaking garments and streaming countenances, we
made our way back to the hotel, and there, divested
of almost all our garments, we lounged in hammocks

and rocking-chairs, drinking iced sangaree and sweetened lime-juice, and smoking innumerable cigars,
until it was time to dress for our afternoon drive.

Killing time in the tropics is no easy matter; and
how we should have spent this long weary day we
know not, had not good luck placed in our way a
file of Jamaica newspapers. The general tone of
these journals— of which we afterwards learned the
colony supported no less than seven—was one of
extreme animosity to each other and to all the world
besides, except that favoured class which they called
"our readers." Some of the advertisements were
especially amusing. Trades-people seemed to attempt
to outvie each other in the absurdity of their an-
nouncements. A livery stable-keeper says :—

"Something may be done! Something can be
done! Something shall be done! Something will
be done! Something must be done! If the prices
are made to suit the times, now come, something
worth knowing. The cheapest stables, at Goodman
Mordecai to defy competition. Carriages and pair
to funerals, at 8s.; horse and buggy to funerals, at
4s.; carriages and pair to wedding, at 10s.; and a
pair of horses for hearse, at 6s."

Another, in Spanish Town, heads his advertisement :—

"Livery! Livery! Livery!

"This is a New Year, and it behoves every man
to turn over a new leaf. How many will profit by
this is doubtful; but as charity begins at home, it is
as well we see the beam in our eyes before we look

at the mote in our brother's. To those who have
hitherto kindly patronized us, we thank. To those
who intend to patronize us, we will be more thankful.
To those who are indebted to us, we beg to shell up.
And to those we owe, we ask a little patience.
There is a time for everything. A time to mourn,
a time to laugh. A time to pay debts, and a time
to trust again ; and as it now happens to be the time
for paying debts, we beg those who are indebted to
us to square up, to enable us to put all square. We
are happy to inform the public that ' poor old Trust '
gave up the ghost on the 31st December, and we
sincerely hope that his heirs and successors will not
pay us a visit. We desire to live in charity and
brotherly love one towards another, more especially
those who carry on a similar business, always bearing in mind that when rogues quarrel honest men
come by their own."

H. C. advertises his umbrellas in the following
style :—

"Umbrellas! Umbrellas!—Papa always told me
to provide against a rainy day, so I have bought all
these umbrellas. The subscriber begs to call the
immediate attention of the public in general to a
large collection of the above article, and recommends
their providing themselves with one or more of this
very useful commodity, so as to obviate the disagree-
ableness of borrowing from their friends during the
rainy season."

The negroes are especially appealed to in the following :—

"Tax Collector Again!—Ow—Dis Money! Dis
Money!! Why Jacob no pay him taxes I wonder.
Ah! Old woman say—'Tan far—see better'—You
no know Jacob yet—him a goin' a Kingston fa de
races, and him putten' up all dat money fe buy
saddle from John Madonald shop by de *Marning
Journal* office, where all de sportin' gentleman buy
harness. Jacob no pay no tax till after races oba'!!
I know it!!! Jacob too trickify!!! But mother—
you know hearie what Judge Blair tell Jim de
oder day, when him beg fa' two mont' fa' pay Massa
Thompson? Him say, *so sweet*, to Jim—'No Jim—
you will be spendin' you' money fa' Christmas and
de races—and you owe Mr. Thompson dis money
now—No Jim! you must pay it in one month.'
Jacob betta' take care wid him saddle. Pay tax
fuss, and buy saddle noder time!!!"

A store-keeper on the north side gives this,—

"Notice — To young men about to marry! A
magnificent brass 4 post canopy bedstead just landed,
will be sold a great bargain."

A dentist heads his advertisement with a ghastly
woodcut representing a set of false teeth, surrounded
with extracted stumps of all descriptions, and all the
instruments of his craft. A house-owner offers, in a
curious misprint, "For lease or rent, that desirable
family country residence, Depass'-Delight (Famished)."
Bitterly sarcastic are some in their terms. A wharf-
inger gives "Notice—There are some persons in this
town who gives a great deal of trouble and annoy-
ance in paying freight per droghers—and dare say

the parties alluded to will understand." A quaint intimation of marriage is thus given :—

"Grey Town, 15th November 1869. Notice.— The undersigned hereby notifies the public of Jamaica, from unavoidable and indispensable reasons, that it is his intention to be married at the above-named place; so that if hereafter any objections be made to the said marriage, they may be null and void.—J. R."

A wife having left her husband's protection, he gives the following :—

"Caution.—Whereas my wife, S. R., having left my care and protection, and is gone home to her parents (refusing any longer to serve me, and thus ceasing to be my wife), this is to give notice that if I find her in my provision ground from and after date—which she is in the habit of destroying—I shall proceed against her as a trespasser, according to law."—P. R."

Of the same character is the following :—

"Hurloch, St. James, 9th October 1871. Caution. —The undersigned hereby cautions the public against giving any credit to his wife, R. H. (an African), as he will not be responsible for any debts she may contract; therefore, whoever gives her credit will do so in their own wrong.
his
J. ✕ H.
mark."

As a specimen of an obituary notice, the following is probably unique :—

" Died at one of her son's (*sic*) residence, B's Penn, in the parish of Clarendon,

MISS SUSAN S——,

Aged about eighty years. For many years she resided and was many years sole manager of her own penn, R's M., in the parish of Clarendon.

" She was truly a mother in Israel, and her remains were followed to their last resting-place by almost all the respectable inhabitants of F. P., and a large number of her own relatives.

" The deceased has left a number of children and grandchildren to mourn their irreparable loss.

May she rest in peace."

The last quotation we shall give is the following:—

" St Ann's Bay, March 14, 1870.—It being rumoured in this, and other parts of the island, that I have contracted a marriage in England : This is to authorize any person or persons who are able to prove the same, to come forward, or communicate with the Inspector of Constabulary of this Parish ; as a safeguard against the public, as I mean to enter into such arrangements the first opportunity afforded me.— W. G. M. B."

Towards five o'clock the town, which had been during the heat of the day like a city of the dead, began to brisk up wonderfully. Jalousies were opened. Ladies in evening dress—low bodies, bare arms, and faces whitened with *poudre de ris*—appeared at the windows, or were discovered lounging on rocking chairs in the piazzas. Carriages, too,

commenced to reappear on the streets, filled with
ladies and children and portly fathers of families
going for their evening drive. As it happened to be
"band" night, we took a carriage and drove to Up
Park Camp, where, underneath a spreading cotton
tree, we heard the band of the 3d West India Regi-
ment discourse much excellent music. We were,
however, disappointed to find only about half-a-dozen
carriages present, and these for the most part were
occupied by Jewesses. Some officers on horseback, a
few pale-faced children seated under a tree with
their black nurses, and a score of idle, lounging
black soldiers in Zouave uniform, made up the whole
of the company. Amongst the latter we were
pointed out several old Africans; and if their looks
might be taken as an index to their character, one
would be inclined to consider them as savage as
when they came from their native Guinea. We subsequently discovered this was really the case. They
never lose their barbarous ferocity. When enraged
they are no more responsible for their actions than
the tiger which has tasted blood. Under a popular
colonel they may make good soldiers in war: they
are said to be rather dangerous customers in times
of peace. The citizens of Kingston—not a very
warlike crew, it must be confessed—congratulate
themselves that Up Park Camp is at least two miles
out of town. To such old savages the restraints of
civilisation are a *gêne* and an incumbrance. Shoes
and gloves are especially distasteful to them. "Barrackie fe handie" (barracks for the hands), said one

fellow with filed teeth and face tattooed with his
"country marks," to a friend of mine—"Barrackie
fe handie bad enough; but barrackie fe footie, tooey
bad, tooey bad."

Town life in Kingston is strikingly sombre and
unexciting. There are few amusements either public
or private. Dinner parties are rare events. The
little theatre on the Parade is opened, on an average,
twice a year—once for the performance of a local
amateur company; on the other, for that of a stray
professor of legerdemain on his way home from
Panama. Not long ago it was taken by an itinerant
performer on the flying trapeze. But the Kingston
press was so shocked by the impropriety of the wife
and daughter of the unfortunate man taking part in
the entertainment, that·after a couple of nights' per-
formances he was compelled to close his doors.

It was half-past seven before we returned to our
hotel for dinner. The fierce sea breeze—which had
lasted all day, and which from its healthful effects
the Creoles call "the doctor"—had died down, and
the "land" breeze had not yet set in. Night had
come upon us suddenly as we were driving home
from camp—for in this country there is no twilight
—and the stars, to use a negro idiom, were "sprink-
ling the sky." As in the early morning, the streets
were full of people. We passed several men with
little glass models of houses brilliantly illuminated
on their heads, yelling out what sounded to us like
"I scream!" at the pitch of their unmusical voices.
They were, however, only vendors of ice creams—a

luxury which, strange to say, is to be got in this burning land at no other hour of the day. Then came by a woman with a basket of roasted pindar or ground nuts (*Arachis Hypogœa*) on her head. Of all the street cries we had heard during the day this was the only one which had either music or rhythm about it. It was a plaintive little melody in the minor key, not very appropriate to the words, it must be confessed. But it came prettily in between the strains of a rattling set of quadrilles which issued from a house on the other side of the road, and we rather regretted when she turned the corner of a neighbouring street, and her

> " Pindar buy, young gentlemen !
> Pindar buy, young ladies !
> Pindar buy, young gentlemen !
> Pindar, pindar, buy !"

was heard by us no more.

III

THROUGH THE LAGOON TO SPANISH TOWN.

WE had grown very tired of Kingston and its heat
and its mosquitoes. We had turned veritable *pieds
poudreux* with tramping over its dusty streets, and
were sick even unto death with chaffering with trades-
men, and trying to induce them to charge only double
price for everything we wanted. It was therefore
with no sigh of regret that one dull grey morning,
about six A.M., we found our travelling buggy at the
door, and ourselves starting on our tour round the
island.

As we passed through the hall, on our way down-
stairs, we discovered the old house-cleaner on her
knees, hard at work on the floors as usual. In the
laziness of her spirit and the stiffness of her old
joints, she was grumbling over her daily task.

"My father! de floor tough dis morning!" she
said, as we came up with our cloaks and umbrellas,
and railway rugs over our arms.

She looked when she saw our preparations for
departure. "Hi, massa! you gwine away, sa?" she

asked in some surprise, "and de day look quite mournful too! It mak me feel quite sad to see you gwine away, sa! Yes!" she continued, in a tone of melancholy soliloquy—"husban's an' wives mus' part; parients an' childring mus' part; how much more de bes' of friends!—Tank you, sa!" she went on, as we dropped a coin into her bony hands, "an' a safe trabel to you, massa, an' me hopes me will meet you in heaben."

"Let us hope we may meet again on earth," we said, the lady looked so disconsolate.

"P'raps, massa; but you young an' me old, you see. Dat mak de differench. But me do hope me may meet you in heaben. Don't you think it will be delightful to be in heaben, massa?—Noting to do, no work, no boderation, no cleaning, no noting; but always to fold me hand, and to sit down chattering with me Saviour. Yes, massa!" said the old creature, warming up into a frenzy of religious ardour. "Ef me did not know me was a sacred girl of the Lord, me heart would quail and grow soft before Massa Lord! An' to tink of de judgment!" she pursued, "when we all shall raise up out of our grabes in a lump! But me bery old, for true. Me fader Guinea man, an' me moder Creole, an' me bery old woman now! Good-bye den, sa! God bless you!" and she turned to her scrubbing and polishing again.

All this time the *dura ilia* of our buggy were being crammed with portmanteaus and travelling-bags, guns, butterfly-nets, and all the impedimenta of the holiday traveller in England. A good friend had recommended our taking with us a supply of "tinned productions," to supply the deficiencies of country lodging-houses ; and if we had acted on all the other recommendations we received, we should have carried with us, in addition to the host of unnecessary rubbish which we did take, such useful articles as a photographic camera, a mountain-barometer, a Norwegian kitchen, wading-boots, a bull's-eye lantern, a large ham, a complete set of ice-buckets, a boot-jack, and a fishing-rod.

By the time everything was packed there was barely room in the buggy to stow ourselves away.

How these two poor goose-necked, fiddle-headed screws—these " soldier-officer horses," as a passing negro *gamin* sarcastically called them, which had been spared to us on hire for the ridiculously small sum of one pound per diem—were to drag this imposing load was a mystery which we vainly strove to solve. But they started gallantly enough, and our hopes rose, as, under the constant application of the whip, and loud encouraging cries from our driver Bob, we galloped at full speed through the empty streets.

And here let us introduce our faithful Bob to the reader's attention.

He was a sprightly enough young negro when first he entered our service, with the features of a baboon, silky wool (for his mother was a French Creole), and a mouth of indescribable ugliness. He was exceedingly conversible, as we subsequently found to our cost, and was given to singing, although

he had neither voice nor ear. So long as he rubbed
down his horses to such choice songs as

> "Ould lady ! lend me your daughter ;
> Five cents go to a quarter,"

or

> "Cherata ! Gordon ! him hang on wire ;"

or even

> "Monkey, monkey, play de fiddle,"

all went well ; and if we were starting for a journey
we could calculate on the buggy being ready in at
least two hours after we had ordered it. But if he
happened to be in a bad humour, or in low spirits,
or if he had had an extra glass of rum and water
the night before, his melody would take the form of
the most *grewsome* chants he had ever heard, and we
knew that our arrangements were doomed for the
day.

Excuses were always ready when Bob did not wish
to travel. He would himself break off a horse's
shoe, and then tell us he could not start until it was
shod. He would cut the harness on purpose to
delay us by having it mended.

His especial weakness was for tobacco and dress.
On Sundays, or when visiting friends, Bob's manifold
changes of raiment were the delight of himself and
the envy of all his fellow-servants. How he managed
to carry about with him his marvellously extensive
wardrobe I never was able to ascertain.

He prided himself on his education too. No
matter how pressed we were for time, he would read
his Bible for an hour every morning, seated in a

conspicuous position in the yard, where he might be seen of men. He was an "inquirer" of the Wesleyan denomination, and but for some amiable fleshly failings would long ago have been admitted a "member."

"But I expects to become one dis year," he said, when he told us all this.

Then in his woody treble he commenced the well-known revival hymn :—

> "Let us go all togeder, all togeder, all togeder,
>   Let us go all togeder to de blessed land above ;
>   Come my fader and my moder, my sister and my broder,
>   Let us go all togeder to de blessed land above."

We had decided to go over to Spanish Town by road, instead of by rail, for reasons which need not here be stated.

The first few miles of our journey were very uninteresting. The country was a dead level. The road ran between hedges of dildoes, with here and there a distant view of the sea glittering like a burnished mirror in the sunlight. For a background we had the eternal hills, on which the shadows lit and fled with ever-varying effects, which would have delighted an artist.

Occasionally we passed a bush of prickly pear, a lignum-vitæ tree, a group of Turk's-head cacti, a flock of goats, or a whirling cyclone of dust. We were glad of anything to break the monotony of that straight, endless, "faultily faultless" road.

Once—rare chance—we met a beggar. He was a wretched old man, perfectly blind, with fleshless legs and great splay feet. His sole clothing consisted of a staff and a scanty pair of trousers. Hearing the rumble of our approaching carriage he flung himself on his knees in the middle of the road, with his lean bony hand outstretched for charity.

"I beg you, massa! I beg *you*, massa! I beg you, massa-a-a!" he cried, in a whining crescendo, like the wail of an Australian dingo.

In England such a man would end his days in the workhouse. Here he can only be placed on the "porpus" list, as the negroes call the pauper list, of his parish, and will probably be allowed to die by the roadside. The coroner will hold an inquest upon him, if the John Crows do not save him the trouble. The witnesses will prove that he was a poor, useless, good-for-nothing waif of humanity, whom nobody owned. The jury will bring in a verdict of "Found dead," and *perhaps* the parish may bury him.

Almost midway between Kingston and Spanish Town is a wide lagoon, from which exhales at night so fetid a miasma that few persons care to travel across it after dark. High banks of bulrushes waving on either side of the road; black pools of standing water, where wild-duck bob and splash; convolvuli weaving themselves into thick veils of greenery, and mantling every tree; here and there a group of water lilies;—such is this dreary, dismal swamp. Of nights, a low-lying mist,—"essence of owl," as the Indians call it—"essence of fever," as it might more justly be described,—broods darkly over the scene. But the negroes fear it not; and night after night come out with torches of split bamboos to catch the large morass crabs, which burrow in its putrid soil. Dazzled and blinded by the glare of the light, the crab is unable to reach its hole, and falls an easy prey to its captors.

About a mile and a half further on is a large ceiba or cotton tree, which has had the honour of being described in every book of travels that has been written about Jamaica. It holds its head very high in consequence. Its circumference is between twelve and fourteen feet. The little cotton-tree sparrows make their nests in its branches, and in the buttresses of its trunk reside a colony of macoco beetles, a delicacy as dear to the negro as the snail or frog to a Frenchman.

There is no more striking feature in the Jamaica scenery than one of those noble trees, which not uncommonly reach a height of from seventy to a hundred feet, its roots expanding into angular buttresses sometimes eight or ten feet high, covered up to the summit with wild pines and other parasitical plants, and with long rope-like withes depending from its highest branches. As timber it is worthless; but the body is sometimes fashioned into canoes, which are occasionally fifty feet long, and capable of holding eight or nine hogsheads of sugar.

" Cracious ! " said Bob, clutching my hand as I was in the act of hurling my stick at the tree to bring down a waxy orchid which had attracted my attention. " Don't do dat, massa, if you please ! "

"Not throw my stick at the tree, Bob? Nonsense!"

"For true, massa! No, massa. I beg you quite hard."

"But why not, Bob?"

"Massa don't understand dese tings : but cotton tree bery comical tree, an' if you did trow dat stick I an' you wouldn' lib to de end of de year!"

Such was our first introduction to negro superstitions.

"Massa eber hear de nigger proverb 'bout cotton tree?"

"No, Bob. I don't think we have."

"Well, you know, ' when cotton tree fall, billy-goat jump over him;' but den de old-time people say, 'By am bye buckra (gentleman's) dog catch billy-goat by him ear, an' mek him cry Ba-a-a!' Ha! ha! ha!" and Bob laughed hilariously at the wit of the saying.

From this till we reached Spanish Town nothing worthy of notice occurred. It was breakfast-time when we entered the dusty streets of the old dead capital of the island, and right glad indeed were we to pull up at the door of our friend's house, and disappear into the recesses of his cool, dark, hospitable mansion.

IV.

SPANISH TOWN, or St. Jago de la Vega, is the capital *de jure*, whilst Kingston is the capital *de facto*, of Jamaica.

One of the most ancient cities in the colony, the seat of government, and once the home of all that was wise and learned and distinguished in Jamaica society, it is now a waste and a desert. Long-tailed pigs wander about the streets; carrion-crows pick up garbage in its once thronged thoroughfares. At the back of the handsome square where King's House is situated, the negroes have built their shingled huts.

Everything connected with it is dull and languid. The few officials whose duties keep them there are gloomy and dispirited; and the occasional balls, which, like angels' visits few and far between, waken the echoes in the old ball-room of Government House, only by the contrast render the desertion more marked and the solitude more appalling.

Yet wandering through its deserted streets one cannot but feel that after all there was a time when

Spanish Town was indeed a city. The very houses, albeit they are tumbling to pieces, have an air of aristocracy about them to which those in Kingston have no pretension; and what we seek for in vain in every other part of the colony, viz., traces of its ancient grandeur, we find in St. Jago de la Vega.

Looking at these antiquated mansions, with the numbers still on their doors, we can imagine the days when governors and bishops and judges held high festival within. What visions of jerked hog and black crab, of turtle-soup and old Madeira, does the sight of them produce! What pictures do they conjure up of those wicked old times when *aides-de-camp* used to ride alligators through the streets, when admirals used to give balls to the brown girls of the town, when vice in every shape was more reputable than it is at present! Is there a single bottle of the old Madeira extant? Does any one remember the the Hell Fire Club? Is there any one alive who has tasted Bath punch?

The old barn-like cathedral of Spanish Town contains a few good monuments; notably one to Lady Elgin, by Steell of Edinburgh. There is an epitaph, too, to the memory of a departed functionary, which we cannot refrain from giving, as an edifying instance of Creole modesty. Under the medallion of M. T. Cicero we read:—

Near this place are interred
the remains of
HUGH LEWIS, Esquire,
Barrister-at-law, His Majesty's Advocate-General for this Island,
and
Representative in Assembly for the Parish of Port-Royal.
He was born the 2d August 1753.
He died the 23d January 1785.
Early and zealously attached to the profession of the law,
which nature had prepared him to adorn,
He cultivated her partial endowments
with unremitting assiduity.
To a voice, clear and strong,
To action, graceful and affecting,
He added knowledge the most accurate and extensive.
Superior, both from integrity and ability,
To the meanness of sophistry,
His arguments at the Bar were rational and forcible,
His eloquence in the Senate dignified and persuasive.
Though by his merit raised with unusual rapidity
To the highest honours of his profession ;
Yet such was his liberality and condescension,
So truly benevolent was he, and sincere,
That he enjoyed the uncommon felicity
To be
Unenvied by any,
THE DELIGHT AND ADMIRATION OF ALL.

Dating back from the Spanish days—and it is
worthy of remark that, with the exception of Sevilla
Nueva in St. Ann's, all the great Spanish settlements were on the south side of the island—the
history of Spanish Town is the history of the colony.
Under its Spanish masters it had its abbey, its chapels,
and its convents; but beside a magnificent avenue
of tamarind trees, which marks the site of the Spanish
Governor's house, and a quaint old bridge across the
Rio Cobre near the Bog Walk, no remains of that
age exist.

Then came the English conquest, with its long bede-roll of names, which are household words in English naval history. In its streets the struggle between cavaliers and roundheads was enacted as fiercely as at home, and a local antiquary, the Honourable Richard Hill, states in one of his works that the common negro ejaculations of " My father!" and " O King!" used to express surprise or astonishment, date back from these times. Those were the days of the buccaneers too. One of them, Sir Thomas (or, as he is sometimes called, Sir Henry) Morgan, actually rose to be Governor of Jamaica, and very odd and not altogether edifying stories are still told of the great doings which used to take place in King's House under his reign.

From that date up to the time when the House of Assembly became a power both for good and for evil in the colony, with the exception of a few negro insurrections, nothing worthy of record ensued. In 1692, the city was severely damaged by the earthquake which destroyed Port Royal, a town which was fast becoming a dangerous rival to Spanish Town—now, alas! like it, a city of the dead. And then began what the Creoles still consider to have been the palmy days of this colony, when great fortunes were made and spent by Scotch and English adventurers; when political jobs were rife; and when the island—unhappy island!—was alternately governed by a knot of needy lawyers, or ignorant, purse-proud planters, just as the one party or the other happened to be in power.

" 'Twas Self and Party after all, for all the stir they made."

Yet even to this day there are men who regret
the old House of Assembly. As for its members,
" the one half," in the words of Hector Mitchell, the
first mayor of Kingston, " could not afford to be
in it, nor the other half to be out of it." " The
brown men ruined it," it was once remarked to me ;
" they were so poor, so greedy, and so fond of hearing themselves speak. They were mostly all lawyers ; and although they habitually lived on green
plantains and salt fish, spoke as if they were rich
planters, feeding sumptuously every day on turtle-
soup and old Madeira." The House of Assembly
was a free institution, and had its black members as
well. One of the most famous of these was a decent
old negro, named Vickers, who was member for St.
Catherine's. He used to ride up to the House on a
dray, clad in a green coat, with brass buttons, a
white hat, and bare feet. Of course, like every
other member of the Colonial Parliament, he had the
entrée into society, and a negro song still commemorates his behaviour at a ball given in Kingston :—

" Den one celebrate black gentleman, de member for St. Cat,
　　Him pop into de supper-room, like a half-starved cane-piece rat,
　　Him say ' him belly pinch him,' so begin fe wag him jaw,
　　Begin fe finding fault, say de duck was roasted raw.
　　Our young man what 'tan by him say, ' Hi ! yerry (listen), Mr.
　　　　Bickers,
　　If you no please wid de vittles, why not pitch in to de liquors ? '
　　Him say, ' me frien', I tink you is right, so if you get any good
　　　　old swizzle,
　　I will pitch in to de grog, fill me skin, and den I'll mizzle.' "

Long before the House of Assembly had decreed
its own dissolution, the fortunes of Jamaica, and

with them those of Spanish Town, had collapsed.
Emancipation, and the abolition of the monopoly on
sugar, had ruined the planters. The old families
were absentees. Their properties, left to be managed
by attorneys, had been squatted upon, and were in
the hands of negroes. The House of Representatives
had become an "unutterable abomination;" and
when the disturbances of 1865 ensued, the Assembly,
feeling itself powerless, laid down its nominal autho-
rity, and Jamaica became a Crown colony. Seven
years only have elapsed, but it is now a thing of the
past as much as if it had expired centuries ago. The
few who remain of the old turbulent spirits have
sunk into quiet respectability. Let us hope that
renewed prosperity to the island· and a bright and
glorious history may be the results of "The New
Constitution."

V.

TRAVELLING in Jamaica has its pleasures : when has travelling not ? But for a country inhabited by English men and women, and which deems its progress in civilisation quite abreast of the day, it has more disagreeables than are creditable to it. In the first place, it must all be done by carriage. There is a short line of railway, it is true, between Kingston and Old Harbour in St. Dorothy's, of which we shall have more to say anon ; but that takes you no more than twenty-six miles on your tour round the island, and occupies three and a half hours in doing so. "Travelling fatiguing in this country !" said a Creole lady to me ; " nonsense ; you don't require to ride. You have a buggy and horses. What more do you want ?" But we do want a little more, madam. Progression at the rate of seven or eight miles an hour is somewhat slow in these advanced days. Sitting in a buggy for six or seven hours is apt to make a man feel cramped and sore at the end of the day. Horses are liable to knock up—Jamaica horses in particular. The sun is rather hot in this climate, too. And your negro driver ! Well, there is such a thing as *bouquet d'Afrique !*

There are a few peculiarities in Jamaica travelling, too, which we may as well mention here. One of these is the number of rivers you have to cross in the eastern, and the number of hills you have to climb in the western, district of the island. In fine weather, and with horses accustomed to the work, a fording or two in the course of a journey is rather a welcome interlude than otherwise. Picturesque groups will occasionally cheer the traveller's eye. Women "kirtled 'boon the knee" washing clothes in the stream, or beetling them on large stones by the water-side; or a "walk-foot buckra" resting under a tree; or a clump of chattering negroes and negresses discussing all the little gossip of the neighbourhood; for "de ribber" is the source of all the scandal, and the generator of all the petty squabbles of the district. But this species of amusement becomes a little wearisome when, as we occasionally found, there were thirty or forty such streams to be crossed in the long day's march. The steepness and ruggedness of the roads is another disagreeable peculiarity of travelling in Jamaica. Many of the roads, in the hill districts of the island particularly, are improperly laid, or rather remain in the old hog-tracks when they were settled by the early colonists of the island. The old maxim, that "where a hog could walk a horse could walk," is only now beginning to be repudiated by even professional surveyors. It was always a matter of astonishment to me how so few really serious accidents occurred on these, in many cases, dangerous roads. One was constantly meeting with drays at their narrowest parts ; or, going sharply round a corner, you found yourself suddenly faced by a wain, with a spell of twelve or sixteen oxen attached, full of hogsheads of sugar, drawn right across the road ; or an ass laden with panniers would start out of "the bush" just where the path wound along the side of a deep gully, into which it would have been certain destruction to have been thrown. And if such accidents were providen- tially rare, this was in no wise attributable either to the carefulness of the draymen, or the intelligence of the animals they drove.

Inns in the rural districts of Jamaica there are none. But in most of the towns and villages are to be found taverns, where accommodation for the night can be procured. There is a strong family resemblance amongst all the country lodging-houses. Your land- lady is generally some old brown woman, the "house- keeper" or wife of its late proprietor. On the walls of the sorry sitting-room are suspended relics of its former occupant—his miniature, done in the days of his prosperity, or his masonic diploma, or his riding-whip and planter's hat, or the blunderbuss he shouldered when he served with the militia. In your bedroom you will find a gigantic mahogany four-post bed, so high that on retiring for the night the assistance of a chair will be required ; the pillow and mattresses moth-eaten ; the coverlet a mass of gaudy-coloured flowers of dubious cleanliness; and the mosquito curtains bearing evident traces of never having been loosened for years. As the evening advances, an evil-smelling kerosene lamp will be placed on the table, which will speedily be covered with myriads of winged ants, moths, and other creatures attracted by the light and the glare. And, in the course of a couple of hours after your arrival, you will sit down to a dinner, of which the *pièce de résistance* will be a sinewy fowl, not steeped in Falernian, alas! but floating in liquid grease, coloured a brilliant orange with "annatto" (*Bixa orellana*), and highly seasoned with "Scotch bonnets," or some other of the many varieties of the "country peppers" (*Capsicum*). Flanking this will be a leathery boil of salt pork, all fat and rind, a green plantain roasted in the ashes, and a dish of yams or cocoas. Creole cookery, always bad, seems to culminate in such houses as these. But if the traveller can put up with bad food, extortionate charges, and a room which probably is not weather-tight, he will be treated with a kindness which, though inclined to slip into familiarity, is the very essence of hospitality, and he will gain an insight into the ways of a class of persons who are fast dying out. Occasionally he may come across a rare curiosity in these "old time" taverns. Perhaps a grotesque picture of the great earthquake at Port Royal in 1692, or a half-obliterated oil painting of Adam and Eve in the garden of Eden, or a musical box, or some "grandmother's" china. Old customs and usages seem to hang about their musty walls. He need not be surprised if his "early coffee" is ground between two stones—a custom once universal throughout the island, and which is said to preserve the aroma of the berry better than when it is prepared by the mill. But if the traveller values a " cool bed" and clean sheets, he should eschew the deceitful allurements of the tavern and throw himself upon the hospitality of the nearest private house. If he is provided with letters of introduction, so much the better; but they are hardly needed to insure him a hearty welcome. Hospitality in Jamaica is a tradition which the poorest planter prides himself in preserving inviolate. Of course, there are planters and planters. In some houses he will find himself surrounded with all the comfort and refinement of an English country house. In others his fare will be even rougher than that of the tavern. " Beef" soup, with the meat of which it has been cooked served on a plate beside the tureen, a " surprised" fowl knocked down as his buggy entered the gates, a dish of " Halifax mutton," as the planters jokingly call salt fish, and a coarse mass of sodden and over-baked " cow meat"—the whole washed down with copious libations of bad rum and brackish water— will probably form his repast. After dinner, the servant, as likely as not an illegitimate daughter of his host, with bare feet, and the universal bandana on her head, will hand him on a soup-plate the freshly picked prickles of an orange tree for tooth-picks ; and then island-made cigars will be introduced, which he will be shown how to light from a piece of live wood-coal, brought in by the same neat-handed Phyllis, stuck on the point of a fork. A breakfast cupful of black coffee, sweetened with brown sugar, and another "long drink" of rum and water will complete the evening's entertainment. But whatever that entertainment has been, the guest has ungrudgingly received the best his host has had to supply, and he would be a churl indeed who did not accept that hospitality in the spirit in which it was offered.

The island of Jamaica is 150 miles long by 55 broad, and contains about 4,000,000 of acres. It is intersected by several chains of mountains, reaching in places an altitude of between 7000 and 8000 feet, generally preserving a range from east to west, and all bearing traces of igneous formation.

These mountain chains may be roughly said to divide the island into two halves, called respectively the North side and the South side. Extensive and widespread plains, lagoons and marshes, prevail on the South side of the island; whilst the North is distinguished by the number of its streams and rivers, the wild grandeur of the beds of its mountain torrents, and the rugged character of its cliffs and bays.

The climate of Jamaica, on account of the varied altitude of its surface, differs greatly throughout the island. The North side is on the whole more salubrious than the South. In the plains and in the large towns the heat is intense; in the mountain districts the temperature occasionally sinks as low as 60° and 50°.

So little does the temperature vary throughout

the year, that the traveller may traverse the island at any time, with equal ease and comfort, except during the vernal and autumnal rains in May and October.

The advent of "the seasons," as they are called, is to the experienced eye readily foretold by the increased numbers of fire-flies and mosquitoes, which seem "to smell the rain afar off;" and by the appearance in the sky, often some time before, of light, cirrus clouds, which the negroes not inaptly nor unpoetically denominate "rain-seeds." "The sky grows dense with visible vapours for some days before the showers fall. As the clouds gather, the coruscations of lightning become more constant and vivid at nightfall. The rains then set in every day, and continue for a succession of days, falling at regular periods in the twenty-four hours. The vernal showers descend amid lightning and thunder; and those of the autumn come with heavy gusts of wind and storms. In the mountains the rains are earlier and heavier than in the lowland country."[1]

The floods during the spring "seasons" of 1868 will long be remembered in Jamaica on account of the damage done.

Many if not most of the river courses in the island are the result of volcanic action, the clefts and rents formed in the earth during its various upheavals ere it finally settled down into its present

[1] Introductory Remarks prefixed to Catalogue of Articles Exhibited by the Jamaica Society of Arts, 19th February 1855, p. 27.

features. Some of these, like the Rio Minho in
Clarendon, which goes by the name of the Dry River,
you can ordinarily cross without wetting your feet.
But during the "seasons" the rains in the mountains
"bring the gullies down" as it is called, and the dry
water-courses become raging torrents, overflowing
their banks and spreading a turbid sheet of wholesale
ruin and desolation over the plains. Roads are
broken up and laid bare to their very foundations;
houses and bridges washed away; horses and cattle
drowned while feeding in the pastures; fields of
corn and cane—

> Sata laeta bovumque labores—

uprooted.

In 1869 no spring rains made their appearance at
all, and a drought almost as calamitous as the seasons of the year before set in. But in 1870 the
"*imbriferum ver*" again brought back, in sugar planters' phrase, "splendid seasons," almost as disastrous
in their effects as those of 1868. In the parish of
Hanover, between Lucea and Green Island, all the
bridges were swept away, and 150 acres of mountain
land came down with a run. In Westmoreland
several estates were flooded, and at Knockalva, in
the parish of St. James, the accumulation of water was
said to be sufficient to float a frigate. At Grange Hill
in Hanover a severe landslip took place, and a house
which stood on the top of a hill was thrown down
completely. "Two large trees," said an eye-witness
of the scene, "which formerly grew near the top of
the hill, slid down the slope evidently without let or

hindrance.   Growing within a few feet of each other, they still hold the same position.   Having descended some sixty or seventy feet, they have been arrested in their course, and now remain erect upright, in the same relative position to each other in which they grew, and which they have held for the last century. Except for the wreck of mud, earth, stones, puddles of water, bushes, broken branches, etc., with which they are surrounded, you would not believe they had ever been moved."[1]

[1] From an interesting letter in Gall's *West India News Letter*, No. 247, June 9, 1870.

VI.

WE left Spanish Town by the early train for Old Harbour—the Esquivilla of the Spaniards—which we reached about nine o'clock. A more uncomfortable journey than these few miles of railway travelling it was never our lot to endure. We seemed to be in actual danger every minute. The train swung from side to side, jolted up and down, bumped its carriages together, careless alike of engineman or driver, acting apparently upon the dictates of its own irresponsible caprice. It would stop, perhaps, to utter piercing shrieks from its whistle—a cow was crossing the line—or, after a sudden explosion of pea-soup coloured smoke, a shower of live wood sparks would penetrate into the carriage, burning holes in our garments and occasionally alighting in our eyes. What with stopping for cows, and stopping to water, with slackening speed when the rails were broke, and with going at a snail's pace over some badly built embankment, it took us two hours to travel twelve miles—two hours of actual physical misery, unalleviated by even ordinarily comfortable carriages, and without the slightest protection from the glaring morning sun.

There was little in the scenery to divert our attention from the disagreeables of our journey. We passed through Bushy Park Estates, through high fields of sugar-canes—surely the most unbeautiful sight, except of course to a planter, which nature has to bestow.

We were struck with the profuse growth of the convolvuli on the low marsh lands between that place and Old Harbour. They trailed over the railway fence; they crept over the ground; they climbed up trees; they made unto themselves arbours of every broken branch and of every forked tree-limb. There was nothing beautiful but much that was depressing in this wild, rank, lavish vegetation. One longed for a little English energy to cut away this life-destroying "bush," to clear the lines and open the landscape. Even our English fields,

"All tied up with hedges, nosegay-like,"

we felt were better than this unkempt, far from grand, luxuriance.

We stopped to breakfast at a little cottage tavern opposite the railway station. It was kept by an Englishman, who told us he had recently been so cruelly oppressed by the law, in passing through the insolvent court, that he could afford us but sorry accommodation. He had not hitherto been patronized, he said. His efforts at tavern-keeping, like everything else he had put his hand to, had been unsuccessful. He had been forty years in Jamaica, and had striven always to deal honestly with the Creoles,

—a dreadful mistake, he added bitterly, as he had found to his cost.

There was, certainly, a great absence of furniture about the establishment. But, *en revanche*, the hall boasted a marvellous work of art—a painting on canvas of the arms of Jamaica, the noble production of a black artist. There they stood as large as life, the two naked female savages, with leering eyes and feather petticoats, and gemmed and jewelled legs, arms, hands, and feet. One grasped bow and arrow; the other carried a pine-apple. Above their heads stood an alligator with tail erect, a characteristic grin on his jolly countenance, and an unmistakably human eye. At the foot of the picture was the motto, " *Indus uterque serviet uni,*" in blue letters on a white ground; and below this in ornamental characters an inch in height was the inscription,

" W. Beckford.
Native Talent."

From Old Harbour we made a flying visit to the " Grand Square," as Vere with its rich quadrilateral of sugar estates is called by the planters.

The road was excellent all the way, but then it was early spring, and there were as yet no traces of " the seasons." The roads in Jamaica, it must be confessed, are but fine-weather roads. The sun is the best way-warden.

We slept at the Alley, a fair specimen of the ordinary and very uninteresting West Indian village. There was a court-house and a market-place, a lock-up like a mosque in miniature, and a quaint brick-

E

built church with a square tower and a slated roof, and a most orthodox-looking weathercock. The churchyard was overgrown with grass and weeds, like almost every other churchyard I ever saw in Jamaica. The Creoles have not yet learned to respect their dead. But it contained three magnificent ceibas, one of which at least, in its gigantic bulk, in the depth of its buttresses, and the enormous length of its branches, far surpassed the famous cotton-tree on the Spanish Town road. We essayed a rough measurement of this old forest giant, and found him to measure no less than eighty feet round the base. The height of the trunk before it split off into branches was between twenty-five and thirty feet. One of its limbs, decorated with half-a-dozen goitres like ants' nests, seemed to reach over half the churchyard, and in the deep embayments of its branches we found some combs of wild honey of pearly whiteness.

Thence turning our horses' heads northwards we arrived late in the evening at the pretty village of Chapelton, among the Clarendon hills.

How can we describe the unutterably bare and barren character of the scenery between the Alley and Four Paths, our half-way station on the road to Chapelton?

Dusty roads, bordered with stunted logwood-trees, for miles; then dusty roads without the logwood-trees; then a dry river-course full of rough stones, which broke our buggy springs and delayed us an hour to have them tied up with ropes and branches; then

more dusty roads and logwood-trees, and then dusty
roads without logwood-trees as before. Not a bird
to be seen, not a butterfly on the wing ; not a bit of
colour, except a stray orchid or two, to break the
drear monotony of the landscape.

I shall never forget the exuberant delight with
which we caught sight of a brilliant bunch of *Brough-
tonia sanguinea* on a dusty logwood-tree in the course
of our day's journey. Its rich magenta blossoms
were a positive godsend to the eye, fatigued by per-
petual sombre greys and washed-out greens. Besides,
we had made a discovery in natural history. We had
distinctly disproved Gosse's statement that the logwood was the only tree on which orchids did not grow.

"Dem bush no grow a' logwood tree!" said
Bob. "Cho! de nigger people call dem trash " (and
he pointed to our treasures), " noting but logwood
bush !"

We rested at Four Paths till the sun had turned,
then started in the cool of the evening for Chapelton.
Here we had plenty to occupy and delight us. The
air was filled as with a mist with the floating flakes
of the "down" tree. Rare ferns grew on the banks;
bright butterflies flitted across the path. If we had
followed our inclination and taken out our butterfly
nets, we should probably have been there till the following day. As it was, the fireflies had lighted their
golden lamps, tree frogs were croaking, crickets and
grasshoppers chirping, and the thousand and one
voices of the night were in full melody by the time
we reached our destination.

We found Chapelton to be a cheerful, well-to-do-in-a-humble-way townlet, standing on the top of a hill and surrounded with an amphitheatre of verdure-covered mountains. There was an hospital for the coolie labourers on the various estates in the neigh-bourhood; a court-house clean and freshly painted; a substantially built church, whose harmonium, it must be confessed, produced most execrable music; one or two good stores, which looked as if they did a little —not very much—business; and some handsome flowering trees carefully railed in.

Beside the court-house stood a splendid Spathodea in full blossom. The top of the tree was a brilliant crown of rosy colour, surmounting a mass of dense foliage, through which the yellow sunlight played, lighting up its under surface and bronzing its dull grey branches.

I carry away with me two agreeable reminiscences of Chapelton: for here, was I not introduced to "pepper-pot" and mountain mullet? Not the Demerara pepper-pot with its evil-smelling and still more evil-tasting Cassareep sauce and its hereditary pipkin; but a rich succulent potage, a very Meg Merrilees broth of pork and beef and fowl, ochroes and calaloo (the West Indian spinach), peppers, cray-fish and negro yam; in colour a dark green, with the scarlet prawns appearing through the chaotic mass not unpicturesquely. Not to be despised was the little glass of punch that followed it; lime juice and sugar, rum and water carefully compounded after the old Creole receipt:

"One of sour and three of sweet,
Four of strong and four of weak."

With the negroes, pepper-pot is a compound of the most heterogeneous description. Prawns or crayfish of some kind are *de rigueur*, but bamboo tops, cotton-tree tips, cabbage, pimpernel, pulse, and even the buds of the night-blowing cereus, occasionally find a place in its concoction.

"You English beat us in our cooking generally," said a Creole friend to me, as we sat in judgment over our pepper-pot; "but you can't come up to us in your soups. Nasty watery stuff! Nothing but hot water coloured with onions and some little chips of carrot floating about in the tureen. Now this is what I call a good soup—something rich and substantial. Birch's turtle-soup is very fair, and his hot jelly and brandy is grateful enough on a cold day. But he'll require to come out to Jamaica if he wishes to learn to make soup to perfection!"

We found this delusion prevalent throughout all the country. Nothing could persuade a Creole that his soups, his minces and his stews, were not the *ne plus ultra* of excellence in cookery. There was a sufficiency of richness in good sooth. Salt butter was imparted with no grudging hand. Peppers and annatto were not stinted. The colouring was brilliant and the pungency intense. But where had all the flavour gone?

As for the little mountain mullet, it well deserves its fame, as the delicatest fish that swims in Jamaica rivers. But it must be eaten the moment it is taken out of the water. Then, wrapped in plantain leaves, or better still in note-paper, and lightly heated on a gridiron over a clear wood fire, it forms, in Brillat Savarin's phrase, a veritable *bocca di Cardinale*.

"The largest and the best I ever tasted," said one of our gourmand friends, "weighed a pound and a half in weight, and had green fat and yellow fat, just like a turtle."

VII.

TO THE BULLHEAD.

WE had but one excursion from Chapelton, and
that was to the Bullhead, the centre of the island.
Following the wholesome Creole practice, we made
an early start of it.

There is something exquisitely beautiful in the
tropical morning. Up to seven or eight o'clock the
climate is delicious. The sea breeze has not risen
yet. The night coolness has not yet been dissipated
by the fierce meridian sun. The sky is of a pearly
colour, white at the horizon, gently shading off into
blue as it ascends. You look out of your window
at a crooked cocoa-nut palm, or a mass of thick
foliage or a glittering waveless sea. Nothing stirs.
Not a sound is heard beyond the occasional crow of
a cock, or the bark of a dog, or the full rich notes of
a mocking-bird, or a jumping dick from a neighbouring tree. Jamaica for the time seems a paradise, the incarnation of tropical beauty, the thing
you have dreamed about whilst sitting over your
fire in smoky London. But only wait one hour
when the sun begins to assert its power, and man's
voice begins to make itself heard, and buggies to
rattle over the streets, and this bustling, sweltering

town, or the gossiping indolent village awakens into
life. Then, indeed, life is felt to be a burden, and
the thoughts turn for relief to winter days and sun-
less skies, and cheery cold frosty mornings.

A drive of about half-an-hour brought us to the
banks of the Rio Minho meandering out and in
through the cane-pieces, and bordered with clumps of
wild canes twenty-five or thirty feet high, their long
arrow-shaped flowers shooting up sometimes six or
ten feet into the air. The ground hereabouts is a
dead level, broken only by the windings of the river,
which in a half-hour's drive we crossed some four or
five times. Passing Savoy estate we came down
upon Morgans, now a deserted sugar plantation,
with its once handsome many-arched aqueduct tumbling to pieces and blocking up the road with fragments of broken masonry; erst one of the most
prosperous estates in Jamaica in the good old days
of slavery.

Perhaps of all the parishes in the island Clarendon can show the greatest number of thrown-up
sugar estates. " I can remember fifty-two working
plantations," said a jolly old gentleman of sixty to
me, " when I was a boy;" and a clergyman who
had been thirty years in the parish could recollect
as many as thirty-seven which had been abandoned
in his time. " I do not think," says Sewell,[1] " that
five miles can be travelled on any road in Jamaica,
without seeing one deserted estate at the very least."
In the once flourishing parish of St. Thomas-ye-East,

[1] *Ordeal of Free Labour in the British West Indies*, p. 186.

for example, out of forty-four estates in cultivation in 1842, twenty are still in existence. In Portland matters are still worse, and although some parishes have suffered more than others the rule holds good throughout the whole island. "It was not always so," said a planter's friend. "It was the Saints that ruined us—St. Wilberforce, St. Macaulay, and their following. Well, I bear them no malice, but would they could only see now the desolation they have produced!" On the other hand, the number of small sugar-mills amongst the peasantry has largely increased within the last few years.

In Clarendon they have quite taken the place of the old estates.

A recent return has shown a total of 5415 throughout the island, distributed as follows :—

Westmoreland,	684
Clarendon,	611
St. Ann's,	611
St. Elizabeth's,	486
St. Catherine's,	657
Manchester,	456
St. Andrew's,	435
Hanover,	364
St. Thomas,	295
St. Mary,	278
Trelawny,	271
Portland,	256
St. James,	411
	5415

Of this total number 5174 are moved by horse-power, and only 240 dependent on manual labour.

But they are attended with great danger, and Dr. Croskery, a well-known medical man in Clarendon, has shown that in spring, when the mills are " about," the number of accidents which happen to the persons engaged in working them is so large as to call for legislation on the subject. The construction of these mills is of the most rudimentary description. They consist of three horizontal rollers, between the first and second of which the canes are inserted by the " feeders," who are for the most part women and children. The canes as they revolve round the central cylinders, have then to be pushed by the hands of the feeders between the second and third rollers, and as these are entirely unprotected, it follows that the legs and the arms of the little feeders are almost as often caught as the canes. If a feeding-board was set up before the rollers, and a " dumb turner" or semi-cylindrical piece of wood placed at the back of the central cylinder to assist the entrance of the canes between the two last rollers, the danger from this cause would be minimized. As it is, there is no doubt that the reckless danger to life and limb caused by those peasant mills should be put a stop to in some way or another.

Oddly enough, that portion of upper Clarendon, in which all the estates are situated, is the most picturesque part of the whole parish. In the other parts of the island the rule is exactly the converse. But all this district looks as if it had been given back to nature. Man has nothing more to do with it. He has freely and voluntarily relinquished it. He has cast it aside as worthless. Priceless though the pearl is, he has flung it from him for any passer-by to pick up. Take the roads for instance. Green sward carpets them, or they are like the rocky channels of rivers,—so thickly are they covered with the stones which the rains of years have washed down from the mountain sides. And as for the mud which lies on them in places—black rich mud, full of decayed vegetation—it was a couple of feet deep in more than one part of the road. "De putta-putta nasty ebery ting up," said Bob; and there was no gainsaying his observation.

But the vegetation would have delighted a botanist. Bright begonias, clumps of wild ginger, Maccafat palms,—surely the most graceful of all that graceful tribe, with their stems covered thick with rare ferns—bamboos shading the river-posts, green moss mantling the stones, and convolvuli shrouding the star-apple trees, and concealing the loftiest monarchs of the forest with an apron of greenery. Nude women and girls were washing clothes in the stream. The little black "picknies" gambolled about amongst their mammies and sisters, equally indifferent with them to the presence of strangers. Sometimes a woman, in an excessive fit of modesty, would take her handkerchief from her head and cover her bosom. But this, it must be confessed, was a rare case. One felt as if he ought to apologize to these children of nature for bringing civilisation, in the shape of a buggy and horses, amongst their sylvan retreats. It

was their freehold. What had the white man to do
there! With his puggree and his umbrella he was
as much an anachronism there as one of these sable
undraped maidens would be in Bond Street.

Then we came upon a little negro village, which
seemed formed as if to illustrate the old Scotch saying, " the clartier the cosier." It was very clarty,
and it looked very cosy. · There was a rum shop, of
course, with half-a-dozen bottles of ale on the shelves.
But there were no buyers and no sellers so far as we
could see.

These country rum or grog shops, as they are
called, are, we fear, productive of much evil to these
little rural communities. The annual license pay-
able for each is £10, a sum certainly not to be
repaid by the rum-shop keeper's legitimate profits
upon " quattie drinks," and three-penny glasses of
ale or porter. Many of them, in consequence, bear
a very bad name, and are shrewdly suspected to be
the depôt of much of the rum stolen annually from
the estates. That they are, one and all, gambling
hells, there is no doubt—for all their deceptive
innocence of appearance. They are the rendezvous
of all the loafers of the district. Draymen, labourers,
petty shopkeepers,—you will see them almost at
every hour of the day lounging over the counter, or
playing " nine-holes " before the door. Now and
then, especially during the Christmas holidays, the
rum-shop keeper, with a view of bringing customers
to his establishment, will give a dance to all the
negroes in the country-side, and the scenes of de-

bauchery that then ensue are almost incredible in their abomination.

Then came another stretch of river. On a bank of pebbles in the middle of the stream, an old, old woman, with a long staff in her hand to support her feeble frame, was drying thin slices of plantain on the sun-baked stones preparatory to pounding them into flour (called *conquintay*) for porridge. By the road-side pine-apples grew wild, and in one or two of the yards were trees of chocolate (*Theobroma cacao*), with their rough magenta-coloured pods growing out from their stems.

At Orange River, where we stopped on the way, we made the acquaintance of a worthy clergyman, who welcomed us with true Jamaica heartiness. He was a rare example of what energy and perseverance could do. He had bought the property on which he resided for an old song, and here, after many years' preparation for the undertaking, he was resuscitating in a humble way truly, but still resuscitating—the thrown-up sugar estate. Old boilers, which he had found buried under planks and rubbish, were being brought out and fixed up in their places. The magnificent old water-wheel, thirty-three feet high, had been patched up and put in order, the cracked and broken gutters cleaned out and mended. The old man was full of his undertaking. He showed us over all his works : his boiling-house with his tache, and his second tache, his "grand copper" and his cooling pan ; his cooper's shop, with its heaps of old barrels carefully collected "from time" to hold his then ungrown sugar. Hopefully and proudly he pointed to his cane-fields. Out of these four or five acres he expected to make a hundred barrels, or twelve and a half hogsheads of sugar, which, at the rate of £2 per barrel, would bring him £120 in Kingston. Each plant produced no less than five roots of canes, and from each of these five roots he would obtain two quarts of liquor. The cultivation of his few poor fields—*mea paupera regna*—had cost him £20; and he had paid £60 more to rig up the old mill, to "put it about," as he phrased it; and now, after years of preparation and scraping and saving to get the money together, if all went well, he hoped to make a decent competence for his old age. Next year he would have twenty-five acres more under cultivation, the following year double that quantity; and such was the fertility of the soil, that he had seen ratoons[1] out of it seven years' old, and after that lapse of time it only required to be turned over to be as good as ever. In addition to his cares as a planter, he was the doctor, parson, and deputy-coroner in all the mountain-side; and if there was a man who rose early and worked late, and earned his bread by the toil of his hands and the sweat of his brow, it was this shrewd, energetic, unpolished, rough, honest Norfolk missionary.

Not the least interesting part of his conversation was his account of the revival meetings which a few

[1] *Ratoons*, a corruption of the Spanish word *brotones*, are suckers or sprouts that spring from the roots of canes that have previously been cut down.

years ago took place amongst the negroes of his district. For seven days and seven nights the people would not leave the chapel. Religious frenzy seized all classes. Some fed on grass; others crawled on all-fours like beasts; others went about prophesying that Obeah was hidden under the threshold of the church. Immorality, under such circumstances, was much more rife than religion.

The hill called the Bullhead is one of the Clarendon range, and rises to the height of 3140 feet above the level of the sea. From its peculiar outline it forms a well-known landmark to sailors; but its chief interest is derived from the fact that it is almost if not quite the central point of the island, whilst it commands one of the most extensive mountain views obtainable in Jamaica.

At first the ascent was easy enough. Our sure-footed mules carried us safely and steadily over the rugged mountain roads; whilst bamboos and lance-wood and foliage of all descriptions shaded our path and protected us from the fierce noonday sun.

"Good morning, father!" said Bob, who was of the party, to an old man whom we met at a shady corner of the road, just where a rope-fall of trickling water lent a cool and drowsy charm to the scene.

"Good morning, sa; hope you is bery well?"

"So so, bad enough," was the indefinite but characteristic reply, "but no so wusser" (worse).

Every step we took was leading us further and further away from civilisation. Clumps of the silver fern began to show themselves on the banks, and we knew from this that we had reached a considerable elevation. Then stray specimens of the golden fern appeared, and we saw several varieties of the superb vine or parasitic ferns creeping over bush and shrub, and hanging in long elegant garlands to the ground. At times a fresh cold breeze came sweeping over the path, and now and then came the " cling-cling " of a black-bird, or the " sweet, sweet, sweet to-too " of the fly-catcher (*vires Noveboracensis*).

Very quaint and very amusing are some of the negro's interpretations of the songs of the birds—

> " liquidas avium voces "—

and the sounds of external nature.

The jabbering crow (*Corvus Jamaicensis*), a wise and learned bird, in harsh guttural tones, gabbles forth

> " Walk fast crab, do buckra work,
> Cutacoo [1] better than wallet."

"Tom Paine, Tom Paine!" whistles out the black and golden banana bird (*Icterus leucopteryx*) ; " Going awa-a-y!" cries the Savanna black-bird (*Crotophaga ani*) ; " Gi' me a bit," says the night or mosquito hawk (*Chordeiles Virginianus*) ; and the white-wing dove (*Turtur leucopteryx*), in protracted and moaning tones, announces that " Since poor Gilpin die, cowhead spoil!" Vain of her plumage the female of the blue pigeon (*Columba rufina*) cries

> " Sally coat blue,
> Sally coat, true blue !"

whilst the male replies, " For true ; for true, for

[1] A small flat hand-basket.

true!" The quail (*Ortyx Virginianus*), like a common crier, heralds the coming of the early spring with the cry of "Green peas sweet!" or "Red peas in, red peas in!" a kind of pulse in which he much delights. The hen-turkey, from which, it is said,[1] our European domestic bird is derived, in melancholy accents complains, "We poor black people hab bery bad times;" and the male, in a fierce gobble, counsels her, "Take heart, take heart, take heart, take heart!"

The bull lowing in the meadow has also his grievances to relate: "Man hab beard, goat hab beard, I hab none; what a shame, what a shame, what a shame!"

The large speckled frog of the morass has a very bad name among the negroes. A book-keeper on one of the large estates told me how on one occasion he overheard a conversation on the subject amongst a group of negroes, who were taking their *chocolata* (breakfast) under a tree, after their morning labours in the field.

"It bery true," said one, "dat Coolie man bring de cholera into de country."

"Cho!" said the head man of the gang, with an impatient grunt, "it 'tan too 'tupid! (stupid). How Coolie man can bring cholera? Do you no know Goramighty send it? But I tell you dis fe true. Dem frog bring de small-pox ya (here). You no see how dem 'tan?" he asked, appealing to his auditors. "Dem no hab mark on deir back ob de small-pox dey bring from dem own country?"

[1] Gosse, *Birds of Jamaica*, p. 329. London, Van Voorst. 1847.

F

The green lizard, again, is the true friend of the negro, and will warn him of the approach of a snake, when tired and weary he lies down to sleep under a tree. Yet with all his love of nature, the negro never makes pets. Cats, I have heard it said, he dislikes, as the type and representation of the evil one; and the lean, ragged, half-starved dogs, with ribs· protruding out of their flesh, that are sometimes to be seen in the neighbourhood of negro huts, are kept always for the sake of use, never as a source of pleasure or amusement to himself or his family.

To animals he is often most savagely cruel. It is no uncommon thing for a man who has a grudge against another to catch his mule or his horse, and after cutting out its tongue and filling the mouth with leaves, to leave it to die in the most fearful agony.

About 1240 feet below the Bullhead, and nearly 2000 above the sea, stands the missionary station of Mount Carmel, a happy, primitive community, very quaint in its simplicity. In the tumble-down cottage once inhabited by the parson we found a dilapidated harmonium and a broken magic lantern, which showed at least some of the means by which he had acquired his influence over his flock.

At this point we began to climb in right earnest; and long before we reached the top, it was hard to say whether our mules or ourselves were most done up. We found the summit of the hill to be an almost level plateau, covered with grass, and ground orchids, and wild starch, and the lovely Bletia, and

bearing in the midst of a little clump of trees a
mountain tarn, at the bottom of which, the negroes
say, a golden table lies concealed. The view was
magnificent. We could see over thirteen parishes.
There away to the east lay the grand range of the
Blue Mountains, with their celebrated peak, 7000
feet high, standing out against the sky. Before us
was a stretch of glittering sea. Looking towards
the west were the Manchester hills, and behind us
and to the northward were the cane-covered fields of
Trelawny and St. Ann's,—"the garden" of Jamaica.
Our toil had indeed been rewarded.

VIII.

A MAN'S estimate of the negro character varies according to the length of time he spends among them. The first year, his opinion of them is a high one. He is amused by their merry faces, their broad grins, their apparent good nature, their seeming simplicity of character. He looks upon them as happy children, for whom the song, and the dance, and the church constitute the essentials of life. The second year his ideas are somewhat modified. He regards them as children still, but now as spoiled children, who give a great deal of trouble ; and by the third or fourth year he has begun to talk about the "irrepressible nigger," and to speak of them in very much the same language as the planters get the credit of doing.

A surface polish of civilisation the negro can attain, and is attaining ; but beyond this it seems doubtful whether he can ever advance. *Chassez le naturel, il revient au galop.* The native springs of civilisation, the quick working brain to conceive, the prompt energy to execute, knowledge of other countries, and of races besides his own, from which to gather

ideas, are wanting to him. Without these, the
negro will ever remain a race apart. It is idle to
compare his character to that of any other peasantry
in the world. He forms a class by himself, anta-
gonistic to many, dissimilar to all. For the Jamaica
negro is the product of many different races, and of
many distinct tribes :—

> " The Jaboos, the Whydahs, the Fantees,
> The Congos, the Warees, the Ashantees,
> The Quaquas, the Sonsees, the Boulahs,
> The Pongos, the Naloos, the Foulahs."

The moral defects of the negro are those which he
entertains in common with all other barbarous races.
Chief amongst these is his propensity to petty acts
of theft,—a vice which prevails to its greatest extent
in the country district of the island. He steals
because he is too lazy to work. As he steals, so of
course he lies ; and, as a natural result, he has little
idea of the sanctity of an oath. Perjury is fright-
fully prevalent in the courts of law throughout the
island. The penalty attached to the taking of a
false oath is, in negro language, " belly swell an' him
die." But kissing your thumb, instead of your
Bible, placing a piece of silver money under your
tongue, or, if a male, being sworn with a handkerchief bound round the head, will avert so dire a
result.

Devoted to sensual pleasure, the negro has little
respect for the marriage tie. Concubinage is a universal institution, and bears with it no disgrace.
The offspring of such connexions—" bye-children,"

" out-children," or " love-children," as they are called,—generally follow the mother.   It is rare that a father thinks himself bound even to provide food for such children.   He bears them no affection : he does not recognise any claim they may have upon him.   If they lose themselves, and die in the woods, he does not deem himself bound to go and bury them.   It is the woman's look-out, not his.   Why should he trouble himself with what does not concern him ?

It must be kept in view that a negro's thoughts, and cares, and feelings are bounded by this world alone.   "It is almost impossible," said a worthy clergyman to me, " to make him believe in a place of eternal punishment."   Death to the negro has no terrors.   He dies because his time has come.   But he dies, like a dog, without a regret and without a pang,—confident that, if there is a heaven, he will find admission there ; and that, if there is not, he has finished his course, and drunk all that he will ever be allowed to drink of the pleasures and pains of life.

Fatalism is in itself a superstition, and the negro is superstitious in the extreme.   A belief in " duppies" (ghosts) is universal.   The spirits of the bad " walk," as the negroes call it, and after death revisit the spots they have known on earth.   They have their favourite haunts too.   One of these is the Salt Ponds, near Spanish Town, a notable resort of the buccaneers in the brave old piratical days.   In the country districts you will see the peasantry flocking

home from their grounds in troops as soon as it
begins to get dark; and after sunset no one is to
be seen abroad. Nothing will tempt the negro to
go out of sight of the light burning in his hut on a
dark night. His fear peoples every bush and every
tree with ghostly forms. If your horses blow or
prick their ears when travelling at night; if, in
passing through a lonely wood, you perceive the
odour of musk, ghosts are either beside you, or near
at hand; if, in some desolate country region, you
notice the faint smell of cooking, the negroes say,
" it duppy pumpkin,"—it is duppies preparing their
food; if a rat bites you during sleep, if an owl
flaps its wings heavily, evil of a serious nature is
approaching; if the wind has a " sough " in its tone,
it is the heralding of evil tidings; if bats cross each
other diagonally in the crimson stream of sunset,
some powerful friend will shortly be at variance
with you; and if you set a duppy at defiance, going
towards it in the endeavour to prove that the supernatural appearance is caused by some undulation of
light, or by the shadow flickering on the curtain-
fold, illness of a dangerous or perhaps fatal nature
will surely follow.

A very mischievous ghost is that known by the
name of the " rolling calf," a spirit who haunts the city
by night with a flaming eye, trailing a long chain
behind him. To speak to, or to touch the chain of
a rolling calf will cause him to turn and rend you.
The only way of escape is to stick an open penknife
in the ground and run without looking behind you!

What may be called the domestic superstitions of
the negroes are very numerous. A belief in the
evil eye is as common in Jamaica as it is in Egypt.
I have seen a woman come into the magistrate's
court with a piece of pink ribbon tied on one arm
and a piece of blue on the other to ward off its
malign influence. It is unlucky to praise an infant
too much or to say that it closely resembles either its
father or mother. To carry a pepper in your pocket
will make you poor. To give a thing and take it
back will give you a stye in your eye ; and no negro
would kill the large black Annancy spider, for
some domestic misfortune would inevitably ensue.
"Trouble," says the proverb, "day da bush : Annancy bring him come da house."

Professedly a Christian it may be doubted whether
one negro in a thousand attaches a correct meaning
to even the most simple ordinances of religion. In
some districts of the island, indeed, these are tra-
vestied at midnight meetings held under leafy
booths erected for the purpose, which are carefully
concealed from the knowledge of the parish minister.
At these "singing meetings" a woman sanctifies the
bread and administers the elements. Hymns are
sung, words are spoken, mysterious rites are observed.
The worshippers grow more and more excited as the
fires burn out and the night grows old ; and the
meeting ends as might be expected in license and
debauchery.

Wakes, too, are fruitful causes of sin. These are
held on the first and ninth nights after death. A

white cock is sacrificed over the grave to propitiate the manes of the deceased; and then ensues a feast or "eating match," after which the mourners indulge in such diversions as "Hide-and-seek," "Hot bran well buttered," "Thread the needle," "Beg you little water," and other boisterous games. Songs are sung little mournful in their character; as an example we may give the following :—

> "Me len' him my canoe,
> Him broke my paddle,
> (*Chorus.*) John Joe, widdle waddle.
>
> Me len' my fish-pot,
> Him tief my net,
> John Joe, widdle waddle.
>
> Me len' him my harpoon,
> Him tief my line,
> John Joe, widdle waddle.
>
> John Joe no hab
> None hat 'pon him head.
> John Joe, widdle waddle.
>
> John Joe no hab
> No shirt 'pon him back,
> John Joe, widdle waddle.
>
> If I catch John Joe
> I will broke him neck,
> John Joe, widdle waddle." [1]

Much the same sort of thing goes on at the meeting which is held on the first anniversary of a death, when his friends and neighbours assemble to build the dead man's tomb. Before this can be done it is necessary "to lay his spirit," and when "it

[1] From "Tom Kittle's Wake," by Henry G. Murray, an interesting and amusing brochure on the manners and customs of Jamaica a century ago. Kingston, R. Jordon, 1869.

runs wild," as is not unfrequently the case, this is sometimes not effected without difficulty. There is something almost poetical in the negro custom of burying their dead in the little yards attached to their huts, underneath the coffee trees and the bananas which they had worked at during their lives. Unfortunately, so far as the negroes are concerned, sentimental motives have nothing to do with the custom.

To our English ideas the religion of the negro too often verges upon the burlesque. The scenes that occur at the native Baptist Chapels throughout the island are almost blasphemous in their absurdity. At a respectable dissenting chapel in Montego Bay, Brother —— was called upon to offer up a morning prayer. "Lord! me da pray," he began, "me da pray! me no know wa me da say: me head is like a well chock-full of nutting!"

"Hi! bredren, you see me now?" said a black preacher standing erect in the little wooden pulpit.

"Yes, massa, we see you!" was the muttered response from his flock.

Suddenly disappearing behind the pulpit he called out "Bredren! you see me now?"

"No, massa, we no see you!"

"Bery well, bredren," he continued, again appearing to his congregation. "An' now my text dis marning is 'a little while an' ye see me, and again a little while an' ye shall not see me'!" and he proceeded with his sermon.

The negro's powers of observation are strikingly

acute although his inferences are hardly ever accurate. In his similes he is often exceptionally happy. Many of them are highly poetical. Thus, when he wishes to describe anything as very light and worthless, he says, " It is like bamboo ashes." Very dirty spectacles are " glasses in mourning for their grandmothers." A deceitful, doublefaced man is said to resemble " an apothecary's knife," which cuts both ways. A pompous boastful man is said to be " big like a man-of-war captain." A determined person is " Mr. Strong-eye :" a boisterous man " Mr. Strongmouth ;" a person addicted to making biting speeches " Mr. Goat-mouth." An ill-mannered man is a " hog-market somebody." A knock-kneed person " has one foot to lay the cloth, and the other to call the company." " Big-eye" is said of any one who is greedy or covetous; " hard eyes" of people who are wilful and disobedient. " Handsome to pieces," that is, handsome in every part of his body, is remarked of an Adonis ; " him favour a patoo" (he is like a screech-owl), or " his face is like foofoo" (like the cracks and wrinkles in a plate of dried corn-porridge) —of an ugly one.

With his nominal conversion to Christianity, the negro gave up the use of the old heathen names which he was in the habit of bestowing upon his children, just as by his emancipation he escaped from the classical appellations with which masters were wont to supply their slaves. Yet, in some of the remote country districts the " old-time" names are still to be found, and a Chloe, a Cupid or a

Venus, is occasionally to be met with. The old African names were fourteen in number, and were given according to sex and the day of the week on which the child was born. The manner in which they were employed, with their general signification, was as follows :—

	MALE.	FEMALE.
Sunday . .	Quashie, cunning.	Quashiba, slender.
Monday. .	Cudjo, strong-headed.	Juba, clever.
Tuesday .	Cubbena, inventive.	Benie, handsome.
Wednesday	Quaco, bad luck.	Cooba, stout.
Thursday .	Qua, ugly.	Aba, strong physic.
Friday . .	Cuffie, hot-tempered.	Fiba, gentle.
Saturday .	Quamin, full of tricks.	Mimba, wild.

Like the Shetlanders, the negro seldom "boders" with surnames. The Christian name of the father becomes the *nomen gentilicium* of the son. Thus, the son of William Roberts will be · named Thomas Williams. His son will become John Thomas, and so on *ad infinitum*. The women delight in high-sounding combinations for their daughters. " Constantia Rupertia," or " Justina Adriana " are common and much admired appellations.

IX

COUNTRY LIFE IN JAMAICA.

COUNTRY life in Jamaica consists of three well-marked varieties, depending upon locality and climate. The inhabitants of the rural districts are coffee-planters among the hills, penners (cattle-farmers) in the interior parishes, and planters round the seaboard. The negro of the country districts is the true, unadulterated, and genuine Quashie. Put him beside the Kingston negro, and the contrast is as great as between the London cabby and the Lancashire collier. His character is to a considerable extent influenced by the products of the district in which he lives. In the neighbourhood of the large sugar estates the peasantry are often a debased and demoralized class. In the coffee-producing districts, on the other hand, they are, comparatively speaking, industrious and deserving. There are few villages in the country parts of Jamaica. The negroes live in " districts "—each man in his own hut and on his own little patch of land. His dwelling is a mere mud hovel, or a rude framework of rotten timber filled in with bricks, or stones. The floor is native mud. Amongst the rafters, scorpions, centipedes,

and other insects abound.   Outside, animal refuse is
stored in some hollow where liquid permanently
rests, as likely as not, to the windward of the dwelling.   The site is probably a hole in the ground—not
unfrequently a swamp several feet below the adjoining road.   This wretched hovel is crowded with
males and females of all ages, not to speak of pigs,
fowls, goats, and dogs; and as the sexes have no
means of separation, the social consequences may be
easily imagined.   The only labour which is cheer-
fully performed by the negro in Jamaica is that which
he bestows on his own " provision ground."   Of
these " grounds " each negro has at least one, varying in extent from half an acre to two or three acres.
Out of this he supports himself and his family, pays
his taxes, and obtains his food.   Like the " plant-a-
cruive " of the Shetland peasant, the negro's ground
is often at some distance from his home.   It is
usually some piece of waste or " ruinate" land, which
he leases from year to year from a neighbouring proprietor.   A provision ground in full cultivation—
" when it a-bloom," as the negroes call it—is a very
picturesque sight indeed.   Within a roughly-made
bamboo or timber fence rise long rows of yams,
twining their graceful leaves round poles eight, ten,
and twelve feet high.   Between these spring lines of
Indian corn (maize), and broad-leafed cocoas (*Cocolabia
esculenta*, a coarse yam), and the ochro (*Hibiscus
esculentus*), with its delicate yellow flower.   Pumpkins trail over the ground.   Knubbly cabbages raise
their bullet heads.   Pease and pulse of all kinds—

the "red Miss Kelly" and the "Black Betty," the "Cockle's increase" (not unlike Antibilious Pills in appearance), and "Sorrow for poor" crowd up all the available space. Clustering over an old orange tree, which in process of time it will utterly destroy, is a handsome cho-cho vine, whose pear-like fruit is one of the most useful vegetables of the tropics; and in one corner is a little patch of cassava (*Jatropha Manihot*) from which the negro gets his starch, his tapioca, and his bread, and from whose poisonous root is extracted the well-known cassareep, the foundation of almost all our sauces. The negro labourer on a penn (cattle farm) or plantation invariably reserves Friday, and sometimes Monday, in each week for labour in his ground. He watches the progress of his "provisions" with a careful eye through all their various stages of "growth" (sprouting), "blossoming," "fitting," "fitness," and "ripeness." Still we are afraid it is true that much of his labour in his field consists of lying under a tree with a "junky" (cutty) pipe in his mouth, indulging in Turk-like *keyf*, and dreamily gloating over his rising crops. The rent of a provision ground of one acre is usually twenty shillings a year. With ordinary labour an annual return of something like £30 may be obtained. The food of the negro chiefly consists of "bread kind" and "salt provisions." The former embraces yams, plantains, bananas, cocoas, bread-fruit, and sweet potatoes. The latter includes salt pork, salt cod, ling, herring, and mackerel. Vegetables are chiefly used as in-

gredients in pepper-pot. Stewed cat is said to be con-
sidered a dainty dish amongst these woolly-headed epi-
cures. The labourers on the sugar estates, both Coolie
and Creole, hunt and eat the large rats which infest
the cane-pieces ; and parrots are stated by Browne, in
his *Natural History of Jamaica*, to be largely con-
sumed by the negroes of the mountain districts, who
say they resemble pigeons in flavour. In addition
to his provision ground the negro often rents a piece
of land as a ginger " mountain," a tobacco " field,"
or a coffee " piece," according to locality. Arrow-
root and cassava are also extensively cultivated by
the small settlers in various districts of the island.
The castor-oil nut grows in luxuriance throughout
all the colony; and as for these, and all the minor
products of the island, such as corn, starch, and
tapioca, he finds a ready sale ; if the negro is yet
inops inter opes, the fault lies with him and not with
nature.

There are two sights which the traveller in Jamaica
should never omit seeing. The one is the weekly
Saturday market of a country town ; the other is a
trial, say, of a case of abusive language in the Magistrates' Court. From early morning, " when day just
clean," as the negro idiom has it, the roads leading
to the market town are thronged with a busy crowd.
Family groups—for on " progging day " no one ever
dreams of staying at home—follow each other in
quick succession. There goes the house-father leading a mule laden with panniers of bread-kind and
ground provisions. He is followed by his wife and

daughter with baskets of pumpkins and cabbages on their heads, tramping along, one after the other, in Indian file. Each woman is dressed in her gayest print and her brightest handkerchief. Her apron is embroidered with coloured threads and decorated with texts of Scripture and moral precepts. Here are a few examples. On one we read—

> Purge me with hyssop
> For I will be clean.
>
> M. T.

On another, below a cocoa-nut tree in purple worsted—

> Open to thee is Paradise :
> Go in and take thy place.

A third bears—

> I know that my Redeemer lives,
> With Joy the sweet assurance.

A fourth—

> 1 am the Rose of Sharon
> And the Lily of the Valy.

But perhaps the most absurd of any we ever saw is the following, which tells its own story :—

> Once the world was all to me,
> But now it turns its back on me,
> O you freckle-hearted young man !
> I lay my eye at Jesus' feet
> Till I find my secret love.
>
> A. P. 1870.

Bringing up the rear is a troop of pot-bellied children —the girls with their clothes tied up high above the knee to give them ease in walking, the boys with fowls under their arms, or carrying wooden trays full of fruit and vegetables. Hobbling along with the help of a long pimento stick, her feet encased in sandals of untanned hide called " sand patters," is

G

an aged crone with a few eggs in a basket, which
she hopes to barter for a little piece of salt fish, or a
" quattie " candle.[1]   Her son, an able-bodied man
of five or six-and-twenty, cigar in mouth, rides before her, atop a one-eyed, tailless, crop-eared, galled,
and sorry-looking nag, already laden far beyond its
feeble strength with two heavy bags of country corn.
In the middle of the road, standing on the sides of
their feet, with their great toes crossed over each other,
two bare-necked women with beaming faces and ivory
teeth have stopped to compare notes about their last
" da-ance " at Mr. Tommy Abraham's grog-shop.
Here comes a trio of young men singing at the top
of their voices.   They are brave, brawny-chested,
swashbuckler-looking fellows, rejoicing in the pride
and lustiness of their youth, and walk with swag-
gering gait and heads erect on high.   The melody
of their song is pretty and quaint; most negro
melodies are.   The words are quainter still, but not
pretty.   Here they are:—

> " Jackass with the long tail,
> Bag of cocoa coming down !
> Jackass with the long tail,
> Bag of cocoa coming down !
>
> Him worry me, him teasie me,
> Him make me dandy leave me !
> Jackass with the long tail,
> Bag of cocoa coming down !"

But we must hurry on, for the sun is beginning to

[1] " Quattie," a penny-halfpenny—the " quarter" of sixpence.
    The negro nomenclature of coins is as follows :—Bill, three far-
things; Fippence, threepence ; Bit, fourpence halfpenny ; Joe, sixpence ; Mac (macaroni), a shilling.

rise and the market opens at six o'clock. Soon the
country town is reached, and the market enclosure
filled with a noisy, huckstering, chaffering multitude.
High in his wooden box, calm and serene, surveying
with the most perfect complacency the busy scene
below him, sits the clerk of the market, whose duty
it is to collect the market dues, to seize unwhole-
some meats and provisions, to decide petty disputes,
and, if he possibly can, to preserve decency and
order. It must be admitted that a negro crowd is
the most good-natured in the world. But "confu-
sions," in negro parlance, do occasionally take place.
The women *will* use abusive language to each other;
and the men, after a visit to a neighbouring cook-
shop, and stimulated by Dutch courage, *will* occasionally buck each other with their heads. But, as
a rule, quarrels seldom occur. Bantering, chaffing,
loud laughing, and loud talking is the order of the
day. By eleven o'clock the last yam has been sold,
and the last bushel of corn disposed of. By twelve
all are on their way home, except those ignoble few
—not so few sometimes—whom business or curiosity
leads to the Magistrates' Court, whither we cannot
do better than follow.

The fondness of the negro for litigation is well
known. Every petty squabble, every trifling dispute, must of necessity be settled in the court-house.
No man so poor but is able to procure funds to "go-
a-law;" none so friendless but is able to induce persons to "throw up money" to obtain for him the
services of a lawyer. Confidential communications

between lawyer and client are privileged in law.
But we think our readers, sitting as a jury, will be
inclined to excuse the following breach of privilege
on the part of a legal friend in placing the subjoined
letter from a " brown " man, only a degree removed in
status and intelligence from a negro, in the author's
hands, as a specimen of the " instructions " which
country practitioners sometimes receive from their
clients :—

"SPRING GARDEN, *July* 28, 1866.

" MY DEAR SIR,—The burden of sufferings to wich
I endured are more than mortal tongue can express
of my uncharitable neighbour, which Sow thistle on
my peace and thorn in my path. which becomes an
anoyance to the Union of Society to whom proff
can testify evedently to be the instrument of riotism
I can assure you that I am almost disgusting of where
I lives and flee to Some other part of God's dominion
for refuge, for my life are even endangered by a
heavy Cloud of witnesses, and the rain of malice and
revenge (as you know that the Blacks hate all the
white & brown people, and Soon put them to the
edge of their Sword.) be poured out on the flesh of
my family circle.   Keep this in mind to be ever my
loving solicitor.   D. S."

But the magistrates—two planters, in white waist-
coats and trousers and alpaca jackets—have already
taken their seats on the bench.   The Clerk of Petty
Sessions has installed himself at the table below.
The prisoner has pleaded " Guilty not " to the infor-
mation which charges him with having publicly

uttered " certain abusive and calumnious language
to the informant against the peace of Our Lady the
Queen, her crown and dignity, and against the form
of the statute in that case made and provided;" and
the first witness is mounting the steps of the witness box. After having vainly attempted to elude
the ceremony of taking the oath by kissing his thumb
instead of the book, or by not touching the Bible
with his lips—in either of which cases all that he
may say thereafter is not accounted perjury by the
negro code of morality—he is at length successfully
sworn, and a dialogue very much like the following
ensues :—

Clerk of Petty Sessions (to witness)—Now, sir,
where do you live ?

Witness—Sa !

C. P. S. (more loudly)—Where do you live, sir ?

W.—Live at Friendship district.

C. P. S.—What parish ?

W.—Cumberland.

C. P. S.—Do you know the prisoner ?

W.—No, sa !

C. P. S.—What ! don't know the prisoner ? Did
you never see him before ?

W.—Oh yes, sa !

C. P. S.—Then why did you tell me you did not
know him ? Now be careful ! Do you remember
the 10th July of this year ?

W.—Can't rightly say the day, sa ! Last week,
Monday—

C. P. S.—Stop, sir ! You must try to remember
the date.

W. (with much hesitation)—It was the 15th July.

C. P. S.—What do you say, sir? Do you remember the 10th July?

W. (meekly)—Yes, sa!

C. P. S.—What year?

W. (evidently much depressed)—1899, sa!

Laughter in Court.

Two Constables (at once)—Si-lence!

C. P. S.—What, sir!

Witness looks hopelessly puzzled, and does not answer.

C. P. S.—Was it this year?

W. (much relieved)—Yes, sa! This year, sa!

C. P. S.—Then why did you not say so at first? Go on, sir!

These preliminaries disposed of, the witness proceeds tolerably enough.

W.—Last week, Monday, I was coming from my ground. Jus' as I come to Mr. Abraham's grog-shop—

C. P. S.—Is that at the cross roads?

W.—Yes, sa! Jus' as I come to Mr. Abraham's grog-shop, I meet up with Henry Thomas, the prisoner. I had a crocus (Osnaburg) bag with bread-kind on my back and my machette in my hand. Says I to him, "Good evening, breda" (brother). He tole me, "Good evening." So I says to him, "Good evening."

Prisoner (interrupting)—What does I says to you?

W.—Hi!

C. P. S. (to prisoner)—Hold your tongue, sir;

you will have an opportunity of cross-examining the witness afterwards. (To witness)—Go on, sir.

W.—So I says to Henry Thomas—" Henry Thomas, my friend, you hol' my bag and make I get a drink to put in my bottle and take home to the missus." Thomas says, " Very well." So I heave down my bag off my shoulder and give it to him to hold.

C. P. S.—But what did the prisoner say to you ?

W.—Please let I make you understand good.

First Magistrate (impatiently)—Yes! yes! But what did the prisoner say ?

W. (sullenly, having been interrupted in his narrative)—He say nothing to me, my worship !

Second Magistrate—What did he call you, then ?

W.—He called me a thief, my worship !

First Magistrate—Well, tell us about that.

W.—Well, my worship ! I says to Henry Thomas, " Thomas, my friend, you hol' my bag—"

C. P. S.—You 've told us all that before.

W. (with an injured air)—Hi! massa! you no let I make you understand.

C. P. S. (testily)—Just tell me what the prisoner said to you.

W.—He said I was a thief.

Prisoner—I deny the question !

C. P. S.—Now give the exact words. Be careful, for I have to take them down.

W.—He told me I was a thief, my worship.

C. P. S. (writing)—" Prisoner said to me, you are a thief." Anything else ?

W.—And that I was too d—n fast, and I was too mannish.

C. P. S. (reading)—" He further added—You are too d—n fast, you are too mannish, or words to that effect." Where did this occur?

W.—Please, my worship, I'm not done.

C. P. S.—Answer my question.

W.—This was at the cross roads, sa! At Mr. Abraham's shop.

C. P. S.—Were you on the high road at the time?

W.—How high road, sa?

C. P. S.—Queen's road, sir?

W.—Hi! Yes, sa! Queen's road, to be sure.

C. P. S.—Many people there to hear what was going on?

W.—Yes, sa! Plenty people was da (hesitatingly).

C. P. S.—Were they quite near?

W.—Far enough, sa! (After a pause)—But not too far!

C. P. S.—What do you mean? Could they hear what was going on?

W.—Hi! Yes, sa!

C. P. S. (to Magistrates)—I think that's all, your worships! (To prisoner)—Do you wish to ask the witness any questions?

Prisoner (to witness)—George Edwards!

W.—Sa!

P.—Remember you 'pon you' oath, sa!

W.—Hi!

P.—Did I an' you ever have any confusion?

W.—Of course we do.

P.—Remember you 'pon you' oath, sa!

W. (to prisoner)—Ax me questions, sa!

P.—George Edwards! Last week, Monday, was you coming from you' ground?

W.—To be sure, sa!

P.—What side you' ground is?

W.—At Content, in this parish?

P.—What kind of ground it is?

W.—Hi! Capital cultivation, sa! It stand well.

P.—No, sa! It lazy-man ground, sa! I have witness to prove dat—I have witness to prove dat.

W. (horrified)—My king!

C. P. S. (to prisoner)—Go on, sir! go on, sir!

P. (solemnly)—Missa Edwards! Is you a Christian?

W.—Hi! That hab nothing to do with the question. Ax me questions, sa!

P.—Answer me the question. Remember you 'pon you' oath, sa!

First Magistrate (to prisoner)—Go on, sir!

P. (with an air of offended dignity)—Did I call you thief?

W.—To be sure you did.

P. (vehemently)—I deny the question! I deny the question! I deny the question!

W. (indignantly)—Don't cross-cut (interrupt) me, sa!

C. P. S. (to prisoner)—Never mind. Go on with your examination.

P.—Wasn' you in a beastly state of stopsication?

W.—My father! What is this?

C. P. S. (to witness) — Answer the question. Were you in a state of intoxication?

W.—No, sa! Never did sich a thing!

P. (to witness)—Did you have any evidence that I did use that low word to you?

W. (calling to some one in court)—Hi! Susan Powell! Mrs. Powell!

P.—Who and who was in present?

Bystander—I deny the question!

Constable—Shut your mouth!

First Magistrate (to prisoner)—Do you wish to ask the witness any more questions?

W. (appealing to Magistrate)—My respectable worship—

C. P. S.—Hold your tongue, sir! (Addressing prisoner)—Do you hear what the Magistrate asks you—"Do you wish to put any further questions to the witness?"

P. (sulkily)—Don't bother asking him any more questions, for him won't speak de truth.

First Magistrate (to witness) — You can stand down.

Witness is retiring, when the prisoner calls to him, George Edwards, did I—

First Magistrate—Call the next witness.

C. P. S.—That's the case, sir!

X.

A BATCH OF NEGRO LOVE-LETTERS.

LOVE letters have always constituted an important branch of epistolary literature. They have been the making of many a *cause célèbre*, the source of many a law-suit, a fruitful spring of pleasure and pain to the young, and sometimes to those old enough to know better, in every generation of the human race. We are a little too much inclined to form our ideas of negro manners and character from the burlesque representations of Christy's Minstrels and others. We are too much disposed to look upon the typical " man and brother " as a boneless, restless, grotesque creature, who wears shirt collars which reach long past his ears, and a necktie of which the bows are at least half a yard in length,—who spends his time in playing on a banjo, occasionally diversifying his pleasing occupation by dancing a breakdown, or crying " Yah! yah! " at intervals. Many of us have yet to learn that the negroes in the West Indies are an earnest work-a-day peasantry, having their own characteristic faults and vices, it is true, and dissimilar to any other peasantry in the world, but none the less real and existent. To many a little thatch-covered hut, half-hidden among broad-leaved

bananas and scarlet-foliaged Poinsettias, or over-
shadowed with white-flowered coffee plants, or buried
amidst tangled "bush" and close-enlaced brushwood,
the letters which follow have doubtless brought pleasure and happiness,— shadowing forth, in phrase
uncouth, nay, even grotesque, to us, but intelligible
and real enough to their recipients, "that long bright
future of which lovers dream."

> "There is no pleasure like the pain
> Of being loved and loving."

Penned after the day's labour on the plantation or
the penn, or amongst the yams and sweet potatoes
of his provision ground, they are the honest expression of the negro's inmost heart, the exponents of
his most sincere sentiments.

I.

MY DEARE LOVE, MY DEAREST DOVE,—I have
taken the pleasur of righten [writing] these few lines
to you, hopin when they comes to hand they may find
you in a perfect state of health, as it leaves me at
preasent. My deare, I have never felt the enjoyment
of love as I feel with you. These few lines is to let
you know that it is my intention of maryin you,
if it agreeable to you. My Deare, my mind is so
taking up with you, I cannot help from righting you.
I am not able to go on at preasant, but in time to
come I hope to be your man of business. Let her
kiss me with the kisses of her mouth, for thy love is
better than wine. As the apple-tree among the trees
of the wood, so is my love with you. Please to say

howdeas [how-d'ye-do] to all kind friends for me.
—I remain, love, your most affectionate love, J. A.
WITE [White].   Answer as quick as possible.

II.

DEAR LOV,—I is wrote you a letter to beg of you
to make me your lover, but you is not wrote me
again.   I is dead of lov every day, wen you look so
hansom.   I cane [cannot] sleep, cane eat.   I dun no
how I feel.   I beg you to accep af me as your lover.
The rose is not sweet as a kiss from you, my lov.
Do meet me to-night at the bottom gate, and give
me your lov.   Miss Lucy toots [teeth] so green I is
like one ear of carn, an' her eye dem is so pretty.
Lard! I wish I never been barn.   Poor me, Garg!
[George].   I lov Miss Lucy to distraction.—Yours
truly, GARG PLUMMER.   Answer me sone, lov.

III.

January, 25, 1865.

MY DEAR LOVE,—I have taken the pleasure of
writing you in time, hopen when it reaches your
hand it may find you at a perfect state of health, as
it leaves me at the present time.   I have seeing in
your letter, my dear, that you wisch to know from
me if it is true Love from my heart.   Dearest love,
if it is not true love from the deepest part of my heart,
whold [would] I set down to write you a letter, my
Dear?   When hear I see thy lovely face, my heart
within will burnt; when hear I absent from thy
face, I long for thy return.   But one thing I did

like to tell you again. do not make it known to
the Public before we began. The reason why I say
that. I heard a certain boy was telling me all about
it, and that only done by you tellin you feamale
friends, whom cannot help; these one secret must
be yours, for this thing is not known to a soul but
I and you and your brother-and-law. Therefor the
fault must be yours. Do not let me hear such thing
again from any body. My dear love, I will be truly
wish that I could maried to you know [now], but if
my life is spared we shall tark [talk] further about
that. My dear, pray for me that the Lord will
speared my Life to become a man, for I truly wich
[wish] that I and you should be one fleach and one
blood. Will you not like it, my dear love? If you
don't wich that, let me know by your letter. My
dear girl, you don't know my love wich I have for
you. May the Lord touch your heart to know these
thing wich I now put before you in this letter. But
I must say that I am doing you arm [harm] for
taken such liberty to write you such a letter as this.
If it is a liberty please to let me know by your next
letter. Do not send me a note again for a letter.
I can not satisfy when I see a letter wich I can not
take me some time to reed. If you had not paper
let me know about in your next letter, and I will
send you some paper. My dear love, at preasant
my love for you is so strong, that I cannot express.
So I even write that you may see it. It is every
man deauty [duty] to write a formil [formal] letter.
My pen is bad, and my ink is pale, but my love will

never fail. King Solomon say that Love is strong as death, and Jealousy is cruel than the grave. Love me little, bear me longer. hasty love is not love at all This is the first time I sat down to write you about it. I love my Dove. Your love is black and ruby—the chefer of ten thousand. You head is much fine gold. You lock are bushy and black as a raven. Your eyes was the eyes in a river, by the rivers of warter. Your cheeks as a bead [bed] of spices as sweet flowers. Your lips is like lilies. Your hand as gold wring. Your legs as a pillar of marble set upon sockets of fine gold. Your countenance as a Lebenon. Your mouth look to be more sweet. Your sweet altogether. I have no more time to write as I am so tiard and full time to go to bead. I will now close my letter with love. I remain yours truly, —— ——. To Ann Williams.

IV.

MY DEAREST DEAR,—It is with a perplexing heart of anxiety that I take up my pen to address you this time, having propos marriage to you. I am now anxious to know the full intention of your mind, accompany with parent. On my side, let it please you to believe me that I am desireous to oblige you in whatever thought or ways that you lik. if you cannot stop up this way, but rather to be in Santi-cross [Santa Cruz], I am very willing to do so. I feel convinced that the merits of your family are not to be estimated by an ordinary standard, and that their most ardent wish is to promote your comfort and happiness. believe me I feel highly honour of being worthy elevated in such a family. In granting me this most agreeable favour, you will, my dear girl, not only dispel the peevish gloom which I am confident will hang over me if I should be deprive of your society. My greatest happiness depends upon your immediate answer. Please speak a word of regard in your parents ears.—I remain, dear Lesia, yours truly love, —— ——. 19. 1. '64.

V.

DEAR LOVE,—I have the liberty of writing these few lines, hopeing that it may found you well. i writ to hare [hear] from you wether [whether] you intend to make me a fool. If you intent to, come before it is too late. If you witch [wish] you can come up, fear [for] I is not an pewpy show [puppet-show], that if you tink you will find any better than me. My mother said that she not understand how you always come here and you not tel her any thin [thing] about me. i witch to send the yam hed [yam-heads for planting], but i do not know wether I will reap the benefit of it. love is strong as death. Jelous is as cruel as the grave. the rose in June is not so sweet. like to meet and kiss you. please to send me answer as quick as passable.

VI.

DEAR ELIZA,—I take the liberty of myself to inform you this few lines hoping you may not offend as often is. I had often seen you in my hearts. Their are myriads of loveliness in my hearts toward you. My loving intentions were realy unto another female, but now the love between I and she are very out now entirely.   And now his the excepted time I find to explain to my lovely appearance [presumably "apparent love"], but whether if their be any love in your hearts or mind towards me it is hard for I to know, but his I take this liberty to inform you this kind, loving, and affectionate letter.   I hope when it received into your hand you receive with peace and all good will, pleasure, and comforts, and hoping that you might answer me from this letter with a loving appearance, that in due time Boath of us might be able to join together in the holy state of matremony.   I hoping that the answer which you are to send to me it may unto good intention To me from you that when I always goine to write you again I may be able to write, saying, my dear lovely Eliza.—Your affectionate lover, affraied [afraid] J. S.   Dear Eliza, wether if you are willing or not, Please to sent me an ansure back.   Do, my dear.

The last we shall give is a genuine negro valentine :—

VII.

MRS. AGOSTISS R—,—I hope you know Valintine is now in seson.   I will take the pleasure to write you this, my hearth is yours and you are mine ; but you do not know it.   I love you as the bee love the flower.   The flower may fade, but true love shall

H

never.   My love for you is a love that cannot be
fade.   You shall be my love here an' in heaven for
ever.   The Rose in June is not so sweet as when
two lovers kisses meet.   Kiss me quick and go my
honey.   I still remain true lover.

XI.

SCHOOLS AND SCHOOLMASTERS.

THE frequent quotations from the Song of Solomon—a favourite portion of Scripture with the negro
—and the use of Solomon's words and phrases, often
entirely foreign to the sense, in the letters given in
the previous chapter, are referable to the fact that
their composition and execution is not unfrequently
the work of professional letter-writers. Foremost
amongst these stands the village schoolmaster, often
himself a negro. A painful desire to air his parrot-
acquired learning leads him into amusing blunders
and exaggerations. Take, for example, the following
letters of recommendation from a schoolmaster to a
clergyman of my acquaintance :—

STOAKES HALL.

REV. SIR,—On my way home last Saturday I met
a Schoolmaster who has been many years a success-
ful teacher. I have no doubt but that he merits
your approbation If he continue to be equally honest
and industrious as he has hitherto been. Believing
him to be better adopted to the Teaching of the young
man Mr. —— with whom you were Entreaty [in
treaty], I have sent him to you for your personal
interviews, as I think Mr. —— whom you were

about given a trial is intrinsically Pragmatic and Enthusiasm in his views of Methodism, and endulge himself in Enigmatic language against the Established Church. A few of your members are Garulity of disposition and also Pugnacious, and if you were to have a Teacher of a Pageantry or Ostentatious nature you will always Inextrically situated. . . . I may add that the retrogression of the W— school does require such a master as the one I am now recommending to you, whose Efficiency I can assured with much Salvific, that through God's blessing, Befor the end of the Present year, your school will again be arisen to its highest Effulgence. Believing that I have now relief of your long wants of a respectable schoolmaster I can only ask for your early reply, and beg to be your most faithful and obedient servant,   C. H. D.

In the following a husband and a schoolmaster excuses the fault of his wife to his parish minister :—

SPANISH TOWN, *March* 15, 1865.

REVD. SIR,—I don't entertain the least ambiguity that the character of a philanthropist which you have when I was at "St. George" has been neutralized, since I hav inauspiciously been separated from you by the direful interposition of External circumstances on which I think from your personal experience saw that I had no controul.   Hoping then that such a character is still manifested by you, and in consideration of which I now presume to commune with you, cordially hoping in the interim my communication will not become unworthy of your notice or respect. From any point of view, I deem I was quite injudicious to have departed from you, but on the other hand, had not that been performed, neither peace nor happiness would I have enjoyed because of the inflexible and impracticable companion I had had to share a part of my being there. I maintain, sir, that this philosophical remark of Mr. Locke is very true—That all our ideas emanates from "experience." I believe furthermore, sir, that people ought to be bold, women be bold, *but not too bold.* Bearing in mind, sir, your Philanthropic character, permit me kindly and with all adequate deference to solicit of you the favour following. Would you kindly give me a recommendation to some clergyman, who you may or might have heard requires a person? Let not my partner's behaviour to self and Mrs. —— be the means of your prohibiting your doing me some service, for I think I can safely assert, *she has re-pented.* "Ira furer brevis est." Permit me to en-quire after the health of Mrs. ——, self, and circle, and accepting my humble, cordial regards, I am, Rev. Sir, your obedient servant, —— ——.

These village schoolmasters are not without am-bition in their way. On a tamarind tree at the gate of one of these hedge schools in the parish of St. Ann's, if my memory does not fail me, I found affixed the following advertisement :—

" English, rethmecktich, and jimmetry (*Query,* geometry ?) taught in firs rate style and cheapes rates by A. B., Professer of the Gospel."

Occasionally, too, they appear before the public as

lecturers, choosing the most abstruse and sublime themes, such as " Man's Moral Obligation to Man," for the subjects of their discourses.   A circular of one of these gentry concludes thus :—

" The Lecturer solicits your kind ﹐atronage under any circumstance ; he is endeavouring by his orations to supplement his means, so as to be able to qualify for a Profèssion in the Inns of Court, London."

One other little scene from the village school ere we close this chapter.   It is early morning.   Some threescore children, of all ages and both sexes, have met to commence the labours of the day.   The negro schoolmaster, fiddle in hand, is marshalling them into classes; and the children—well! it was a Baptist School in a very remote part of the country—are taking their places to the following hymn :—

"Come, Jesus with the shining face,
. Come down and bless thine infant race,
We all assembled shall be there
At half-past nine, at the hour of prayer."

The hymn over, the schoolmaster lays aside his violin, and proceeds to read aloud an exercise in dictation to his elder pupils.   The passage which he has selected describes the sufferings of a goat pursued by the hunters.   The pedagogue's voice swells and rolls delightedly over the long many-syllabled words. As he warms to his work his emphasis grows more marked, his gestures more abundant; and ludicrous is his air of self-satisfaction when at last he closes his book with the words " and, thus happily eluding his fate, the goat soat (sought) and found an asylum, in a sequestrated spot."

XII.

ANNANCY STORIES.

REFERENCE has frequently been made in the preceding pages to the popular tales—the Annancy stories—of the negroes in Jamaica. Corresponding to the fairy tales of more northerly regions, they have been the delight and the amusement of many a generation of young Creoles, white, black, brown, and yellow. Nor, indeed, have they wanted admirers amongst children of a larger growth. No pleasanter picture of peasant comfort and enjoyment is to be seen in Jamaica than that of a circle of negroes seated around some village story-teller as he recounts the cunning and exploits of Annancy.

The chief repositories of this traditional literature are children and old women. It is essentially the literature of a race, not of a nation. Essentially a child of the soil, its subjects are almost exclusively drawn from the common daily incidents of a country life. " It scarcely ever rises above Gungo peas and Afoo yams. It reflects the inward feeling and outward circumstances of a very simple and a very unpolished peasantry." [1]

[1] From an admirable Paper on Negro Literature in the Transactions of the Jamaica Royal Society of Arts and Agriculture. New Series, vol. i. No. 4, p. 64.

The principal hero of this autochthonic literature
is the large black Annancy spider. He is the per-
sonification of cunning and success—two qualities
which have an especial charm for the negro mind.[1]
" He is the Jove, the Thor, the Bramah of negro
mythology. His great strength is in his cunning,
and in his metamorphic versatility ; he out-Proteuses
Proteus. His parentage is utterly unknown—nor
indeed does it seem referred to in any of the Annancy stories."[2] The other personages who figure
in the tales are Annancy's wife Crookie, and Tacooma his reputed son. "Tacooma is a person quite
by himself. He seems without parallel in any other
mythology. He helps his father or not, as he thinks
fit. He is stronger than his father, but has less
cunning ; and when he, the strong, and the father,
the cunning, do unite, woe to the victim they attack !
As regards Annancy and his wife, they engage in

[1] The philosophy of these stories is well explained by Dr. Da-
sent in his Norse Tales: "They are called ' Ananzi Stories,' because so many of them turn on the feats of Ananzi, whose character is a mixture of ' the Master-thief,' and of ' Boots ;' but the
most curious thing about him, is that he illustrates the Beast Epic
in a remarkable way. In all the West Indian Islands, ' Ananzi' is
the name of spiders in general, and of a very beautiful spider with
yellow stripes in particular. The Negroes think that this spider is
the ' Ananzi' of their stories, but that his superior cunning enables
him to take any shape he pleases. In fact, he is the example which
the African tribes, from which these stories came, have chosen to
take as pointing out the superiority of wit over brute strength.
In this way they have matched the cleverness and dexterity of the
Spider against the bone and muscle of the Lion, invariably to the
disadvantage of the latter."—*Introduction to Appendix*, p. 485.

[2] "Negro Literature"—*Trans. Jamaica Royal Soc.*, vol. i. p. 65,
new series.

squabble, which, had the pair been human, might have led them to the Divorce Court, but which, for matrimonial objurgation, are fit to rank with those splendid 'passages' between Jupiter and Juno."[1]

Many of the Annancy stories exist only as pointless, disjointed, mutilated fragments. Others of them break off abruptly just when the interest has reached its highest point.

The specimens which follow have been taken down from the lips of the narrators. Much of their dramatic effect must, of necessity, be lost in their transcription. The action, the imitation of Annancy's drawl, the alternation of tones by which the various personages are distinguished, the little fragments of song introduced, it was of course impossible to reproduce. To have given them too, in all the baldness of the negro dialect, would have rendered them unintelligible to the English reader. Still we trust that we have deprived them of no part of their essential character.

Without further preface, therefore, here follows the legend of

Annancy and the Tiger.

Once upon one time, long before Queen Victoria come to reign over we, Annancy and Tiger were both courting de same young lady. Dey was both bery jalous of each other. So when Annancy one day go to dis lady's yard, him say to her dat Tiger was noting better dan his father's old riding-horse.

[1] " Negro Literature," *ut supra*, p. 65.

Little time after Tiger come to call 'pon him sweet-
heart. But de young lady say to him, "Go 'long,
sa! How can you come courting me when you
know you is noting but Missa Annancy's father's
old riding-horse ?"

"Warra!" cried Tiger, "who tell you dis one
great big lie ?"

"Hi!" said de lady, "is dis a way to speak to
me ? Go 'long wid you, you old good-for-noting
jackass riding-horse!"

"My fader!" said Tiger, "what is dis ? It favour
like you have a suspich 'pon me, ma'am. (It looks as
if you were suspicious of me.) But I tell you, ma'am,
what I will do. I will go straight 'long to Breda
(Brother) Annancy, an' make him to tell me what
time I eber turn his fader's old jackass riding-horse."

So de lady say to him, "Well, go 'long, sa!"

Then Tiger take up him stick, and him stick him
junky pipe in his cheek, and go straight to Annancy's
yard. When him get there, he found Annancy lying
in his bed down with fever. So him lift de latch,
and call out, "Breda Annancy! Breda Annancy!"

Annancy hear him bery well; but him jus' say,
so soft, "Dear Tiger, you call me ?"

Tiger reply, "Yes, I call you. I come to you. I
want to hear good from you to-day, because lady tell
me you say I noting but your fader's old jackass
riding-horse, and I come to make you prove it."

"Hi!" said Annancy, "don't you see I hab fever ?
My stomach pain me bad, an' I hab jus' taken doctor's medicine!"

"Cho!" replied Tiger.

"After I hab jus' eaten two pills, Breda Tiger, how you think I can go to de lady yard to prove that rude word to-night?".

"I don't want to hab any conconsa (argument) wid you, Breda," replied Tiger, "but you mus' jus' show the lady dis night when I turn you fader old jackass riding-horse."

"O king!" cried Annancy, "an' dis cataplasm upon my breast, it burn me so! Howsomever, I will try to go wid you to de lady."

Then Tiger say, "Well, Breda, since you so kind, don't mind; I will carry you on my back."

"Wait a minute, den, Breda, an' I will try to rise out of my bed."

But him fall back. Den him cry out, "Dear! I can't get up at all. Do, I beg you, Breda, come raise me up." Tiger raised him up.

So when Annancy rise up, him go to the rafter, and take down him saddle.

"Hi!" said Tiger, "what you going to do wid dat?"

"Jus' to put it upon your back, Breda, for me to sit down soft, becausing you see I am well sick."

"Neber mind, den," said Tiger, "put it on."

Then Annancy got his bridle and reins.

"Hi!" said Tiger, "an' what are you going to do wid dat?"

"Jus' to put 'pon your mouth, Breda, to pull you up when you walk too fast."

"All right," said Tiger, "put dem on."

Then Annancy took out his horse-whip.

"Hi!" said Tiger, "an' what are you going to do wid dat?"

"When fly come 'pon your ear, Breda, I will take dis whip and lick it off."

Tiger say, "Well, take it."

Then Annancy put on his spurs.

"Hi!" said Tiger, "what are you going to do wid dat?"

"When fly come 'pon your side, Breda, I will touch dem wid my spur, an' make them fly off."

"Nebber mind, den," said Tiger, "put them on."

Then Annancy called out, "Now, den, Breda Tiger, stoop down, an' let I mount you." So Tiger stooped down, an' Annancy mounted 'pon him back. Tiger den began to walk off.

But as him walk too fast, Annancy pull him up wid de bridle.

"Stop, Breda! take time; my head hurt me so!"

Tiger went on till he go a mile. In a little, Annancy take him horse-whip and fetch Tiger a lick on the ear.

"Hi!" said Tiger, "what dat fo, sa?"

"Cho!" replied Annancy, "what a 'tupid fly! Shoo, you fly!"

"All right, Breda," said Tiger, "but nex' time don't lick so hot."

Tiger go on again for anoder mile. Then Annancy stick his spur into his side.

Tiger gabe one big jump, and cry out, "Warra! what dat?"

"Dem bodersome flies, Breda; dey bite your side so."

Then Tiger go on for another half-mile, till he come to the lady's yard.

Now de lady's house had two doors, a front one and a back one. Just as he came to de entrance of de yard, Annancy rise up in him saddle, like how jockey run race on Kingston racecourse, and him take out him whip and him lash Tiger well.

"Hi!" cried Tiger, "you lick too hot!" But Annancy lash him up the more, till Tiger gallop. Then Annancy took his spurs and stuck dem into Tiger's side, till he drove him right up to de lady's door-mouth.

Then Annancy took off his hat, an' waved it above his head, and say to the lady, who was standing at the door, "Hi! Missis, me no tell you true dat dis Tiger noting but my fader's old riding-horse?" So him leap off Tiger, and go into de lady's house. But Tiger gallop off, and never was heard of no more.

Many of the Annancy stories serve to illustrate natural facts. In the following, for instance, the baldness of head of the Carrion Crow or Turkey Buzzard is amusingly illustrated. These vultures, the scavengers of tropical cities, cannot fail to attract the attention of the traveller, almost upon his first arrival in Jamaica. So useful are they deemed to be by the Creoles that a local Act inflicts a fine upon any person who kills one. Their sense of smell is exquisite; and it is stated as a curious fact, that during the so-called Rebellion of 1865, the island was deserted by the John Crows, except in the parishes of St. Thomas and Portland, where the frightful scenes of carnage and of slaughter were being enacted.

Why the John Crows have Bald Pates.

᾽ In a before time there libed a man who hated de John Crows and wanted to destroy dem. But howsomdever him neber get de opportunity, an' de John Crows still libed to vex him.

But John Crow tink himself dandy man, an' it griebe him heart to tink that after all him had neber been christened. So him call a meeting of all him frien' an relation, an' dey resolve to go ask man to christen him an' gib him a name.

When man hear this he rejoice greatly, an' him say to himself, " Cunny (cunning) better dan 'trong (strength). Now I will hab my vengeance 'pon my enemies."

So him appoint a day, an' him tell John Crow to mek a feast, an' to kill a big hog, an' to buy a little rum an' a little port-wine, an' plenty of salt fish an' yam an' oder vittles.

On de day him name all de John Crows of dat country gadered demselves togeder. And one brought beef, an' anoder brought ham, an' anoder a sucking pig, an' anoder fowls; an' dere was yams and cocoas, an' sweet potatoes, an' ebryting, an' plenty of liquor.

An' when de man com to de place where de eating match was to be, him bring wid him a big barrel

full of American flour, which him said was him con-
tribution to do feast. Den all de John Crows clapped
doir wings wid joy, an' said: " Hi! de good buckra!"
But de man only smile to himself an' say, "'To-day
fe me, to-morrow fe you;' 'When fowl merry, hawk
catch him chicken;' 'Hide fe me, talk fe you;'
'You shake my han', but you no shake my heart!'"[1]
Then him turn to de John Crows and say, " When
you hab plenty you boil pot," an' he bid dem light
a fire, for he said he would need to boil de flour an'
water togeder to make a grand cake for de christening.

When de barrel of flour was empty an' de flour
an' de water was boiling, bubblin' up 'pon de fire,
he call all de John Crows roun' him an' say, " You
see dis barrel ya (here)?"

Dey all say, " Yes, we see it."

" Bery well," he say, " come roun' an' put all you
heads into it, an' you musn' lif' up your head or look
roun' till I tell you, fo I hab someting secret to mek
ready fe de christening." So dey all put deir head
into de barrel, an' de barrel was chockful of deir head.

Den de man took de cauldron of boilin' water an'
him step up behind dem softly, softly, an' den he
lift up de pot an' pour all de boiling stuff 'pon deir
heads, an' him laugh an' him say, " Dead fe true!
Dis is de way I christen you, John Crow!"

But after all dey was not dead. Only when dey
got better dey found all deir head peel (bald) where
de boilin' water fell 'pon dem.

An' dis is why John Crows hab bald pates to dis day.

[1] Negro proverbs.

Of the same kind is the story entitled

Why Hawks eat Fowls.

Long time ago Fowl was Hawk's mother. One
day Hawk was going to him work when he see little
Ground Dove playing on a flute, and singing so sweet,

" Fee, fee, fee tender !"[1]

" Marning, Ground Dove," said Hawk.

" Marning, sa," him reply, " how you is to-day ?,"

" So-so, I tank you.   Hi ! what a pretty ting dat
is you play 'pon you flute !"

" Tink so, sa ?" said Ground Dove; an' him put
up him flute to him mouth an' play again,

" Fee, fee, fee tender !"

" Do, I beg you, len' me you' flute, cousin Ground
Dove.   It soun' so sweet."

But Ground Dove say, " No, cousin, me could n'
do it."

" Hi !" say Hawk, " you so quarry-quarry[2] you
no let I mek my old moder Fowl hear you flute ?"

" No, cousin," answer Ground Dove.   " You no
know what de old-time people say, " 'Pider (Spider)
an' fly no mek good bargains !   I could n' do it, sa,
I could n' do it."

Den Hawk spring 'pon Ground Dove, an' tear up
him feathers, an' mash him up wid him beak, an'
lef (leave) him fe dead 'pon de dirt.[3]   An' him take
away him flute, an' so carry away go home.

---

[1] An imitation of the note of the ground dove.
[2] Quarrelsome.   [3] Earth—ground.

An' when Hawk come to him house he go into him hall to de ches' ob drawers dat stan' da, an' him open de one drawer, de two drawer, de tree drawer, de four drawer, de five drawer, de six drawer, till him come to de twelve drawer; an' him put de flute into de twelve drawer, an' come back sit down.

Den he turn to him moder Fowl an' say, " Grandie, if any come to you, ask you fe give him de flute me put in de twelve drawer, you is not to give it him. Yerry?" (do you hear?) An' him moder say, " Yes, sa! me hear." Den Hawk say, " An', Grandie, you mus' hab my breakfas' ready an' keep him hot till me come back from de field. Yerry?"

An' him moder say, " Yes, sa ! me yerry."

Den Hawk take up him hoe an' him machette an' go to him ground.

But all dis time little Ground Dove had followed Hawk, an' when him tell him moder where him put de flute, him listen behin' de door, an' hear what him did say.

So when Hawk gone, Ground Dove come out from behin' de door, an' go into Hawk's house. By dis time Grandie fowl done cook Hawk breakfas', an' was sitting aside de kitchen fire smokin' her pipe.

" Good-day, godmother," said Ground Dove.

" Good-day, my dear."

" Godmother," said Ground Dove, " Cousin Hawk sent me to tell you to gib me him breakfas' to carry to him in de field, and de flute which him put in de twelve drawer to make him play an' sing."

But Fowl say, " Go long wid you, pickny ! You

I

tell me one big story—me no go give you one ting."

Ground Dove begin to cry. Den him say, "God-mother, you tink a little ting like me would tell you such a lie? No, ma'am! me wouldn' do it; me wouldn' do it."

But Fowl still sit by de fire an' smoke him pipe.

Ground Dove cry more.

Den Fowl get angry and say, "Hi! Cho! you too foolish. Don't winka-winka at me (neigh like a horse). Go long wid you, Cho!"

But Ground Dove cry on still.

"Cho!" said Fowl, "it 'tan too 'tupid" (The matter is too absurd).

But Ground Dove go on cry so bad dat at las' Fowl get terrify. Den she rise up from her seat, take de flute from de drawer, and gib it, wid de breakfas', to Ground Dove, fe go carry it to Hawk in him field. Ground Dove dry him eyes, put him flute to him mout' an' play so sweet,

"Fee, fee, fee tender,"

and so go leave de house.

As him went along him eat Hawk's breakfas', but him take de flute an' hide him under him wing till him come to a *lignum vitæ* bush close by where Hawk was at work in him field. Then him took out him flute, and begin to play

"Fee, fee, fee tender,"

again.

Hawk heard him. Hi! but him well warify (in a great passion) when him yerry dis. Him throw down him hoe, an' him throw down him machette, an' him curse him moder for a " cra-cra " (careless), " bogro-bogro" (coarse), " takro-takro" (ugly), " chaka-chaka" (disorderly), " buffro-buffro" (clumsy), "wenya-wenya" (meagre), " nana" (old woman); an' him stalk away out of him ground to him moder house.

. When him come to de yard him call out, " Moder!" But him moder no answer him. She was afraid. Den him walk into de house, an' him go up to de ches' ob drawers, an' him open de one drawer, an' de two drawer, de tree drawer, de four drawer, de five drawer, de six drawer, till him come to de twelve drawer. But him no find him flute. Den him cross de yard, an' step up to him moder, an' say, " Hi! ma'am, you gib my flute to Groun' Dove, do you ? Where my breakfas' ?"

But him moder no answer him. She was afraid.

So Hawk say, " Yerry, ma'am ? where my break-fas', ma'am ?"

Den him moder fall down a' him feet an' say, " Sa! You no' sen' little Ground Dove ya (here), make I gib him you breakfas' fe go carry to you in de field, and you flute fe mak you play an' sing ?"

" You tief!" said Hawk, " me neber sen' any one ya !"

" Wi! O me moder me dead!" [1] cry out poor Fowl.

But Hawk reply, " You tief, you witch! you shall be my breakfas' !"

Den him pounce 'pon Fowl, an' shake her, an' tear

---

[1] An exclamation implying great fear and personal danger.

her till her dead : an' den him eat her for him
breakfas' !"

An' dis is why eber since Hawks eat Fowls.

Of the same character is the tale known by the
title —

Why Toads walk on Four Legs.

Once upon a time dere was a Prince, an' him rich
—hi! him so rich him fling 'way money as if it had
been a rockatone (stone) : an' him so proud dat him
say dere neber was woman good 'nough fo him fe
marry. Now dere lib close to him an ole ole witch,
an' her name was Recundadundundadrumunday. An'
when him[1] (she) hear what Prince say, him make up
him mind fe marry him. So she borrow a silk dress
and a carriage and horses, and when she walk into
de carriage her dress go " shwee, shwee, shwee," an'
eberybody turn fe look after him. Hi! but she
look beautiful fe true! An' when de Prince see her
in her carriage, him cry out wid delight an' say,
" O de young lady is come at last fe me fe marry ! "
But de ole witch threw herself back in de carriage,
an' wouldn' look at him.

Howsomeber, after a time dey make it up all right,
an' de wedding day was fix, and a fat hog kill, an'
de wedding cake bought, an' eberyting.

Now at dis time Toad was buckra gentleman, an'

---

[1] The personal pronouns feminine and neuter are almost unknown in negro phraseology. We have introduced them in these
tales once or twice to render their language more intelligible to the
English reader.

him walk 'pon two leg, an' him had his hat stuck a' one side of his head, an' a long tail coat, an' high-heel boot, an' his shirt collar 'tan' up like a jackass donkey mane. An' him smoke cigar all day, an' when him walk him boot go " quee, quee !"

So him go to de Prince, an' him tell him dat de young lady him a going fe marry was noting but an ole witch, an' her name was Recundadundunda-drumunday.

So de Prince went an' see de young lady, an' tell him that him couldn' marry him.

Hi ! de ole witch get angry ! Him knock off him silk dress : him tie on him junky (short) blue frock roun' him waist, him stick him broken pipe in a one side of him mouth, and him fling him mortar stick over him shoulder, an' go 'long fe find out who tell de Prince dis ting.

An' on de road him meet up wid a cow, an' him say, " You, cow ! you, cow ; was it you dat call me Recundadundundadrumunday ?"

But him say, " No, missus ! me wouldn' do sich a thing."

Den him went on an' him meet a sheep, an' him say, " You, sheep ! you, sheep ! was it you dat call me Recundadundundadrumunday ?"

But him say, " No, Missus ! Me wouldn' do sich a thing !"

Den him meet up wi' Toad. An' Toad say, " How d'ye, Missus ? Hi ! if it isn' my ol' frien' Recundadundundadrumunday !"

An' when de ole witch hear dis, him know who it was who tell de Prince. So him run up 'pon him, an' him take him mortar stick, an' beat Toad till him lie down like dead.

An' dat why Toads walk on four legs to dis day.

XIII

OBEAH.

OF all the motive powers which influence the negro character, by far the most potent, as it is also the most dangerous, is that of Obeah.

"Obeah in Jamaica," says Mr. Beckford Davis, in his evidence before the Royal Commission,[1] "is a twofold art. It is the art of poisoning, combined with the art of imposing upon the credulity of ignorant people by a pretence of witchcraft." The obeah man or woman is one of the great guild or fraternity of crime. Hardly a criminal trial occurs in the colony in which he is not implicated in one way or another. His influence over the country people is unbounded. He is the prophet, priest, and king of his district. Does a maiden want a charm to make her lover " good " to her? does a woman desire a safe delivery in child-birth? does a man wish to be avenged of his enemy, or to know the secrets of futurity?—the obeah-man is at hand to supply the means and to proffer his advice. Under the style and title of a " bush doctor," he wanders from place

[1] Jamaica Royal Commission, 28th day, p. 521.

to place, exacting " coshery " from his dupes on all
hands : supplied with food by one, with shelter by
another, with money by a third, denied nought, from
the mysterious terror with which he is regarded, and
refused nothing from fear of the terrible retribution
which might be the consequences of such a rash act.
His pretensions are high: but he has means at hand
to enforce them. He can cure all diseases; he can
protect a man from the consequences of his crime ;
he can even reanimate the dead. His knowledge
of simples is immense. Every bush and every tree
furnishes weapons for his armoury. Unfortunately,
in too many instances more potent agents are not
wanting to his hand. His stock-in-trade consists of
lizards' bones, old egg-shells, tufts of hair, cats' claws,
ducks' skulls, an old pack of cards, rusty nails, and
things of that description. " Grave-dirt," that is,
earth taken from where a corpse has been buried, is
also largely used. " It is supposed that if an obeah-
man throws it at a person he will die." [1]   But ground
glass, arsenic, and other poisons, are not unfrequently
found among the contents of the obeah-man's " puss-
skin" wallet; and it is not difficult to conjecture for
what purposes these are employed.

As an outward and visible sign of his power, the
obeah-man sometimes carries about with him a long
staff or wand, with twisted serpents, or the rude
likeness of a human head carved round the handle.
He has his cabalistic book, too, full of strange characters, which he pretends to consult in the exercise

[1] Mr. Davis's Evidence, Royal Commission, p. 522.

of his calling. One of these is now in my posses-
sion. It is an old child's copy-book, well thumbed
and very dirty. Each page is covered with rude
delineations of the human figure, and roughly-traced
diagrams and devices. Between each line there runs
a rugged scrawl, intended to imitate writing. The
moral precepts engraved at the head of each page
seem strangely out of place with the meaningless
signs and symbols which occupy the remainder of its
space.

There is something indescribably sinister about
the appearance of an obeah-man, which is readily observed by persons who have mixed much with the
negroes. With a dirty handkerchief bound tightly
round his forehead, and his small, bright, cunning
eyes peering out from underneath it, he sometimes
visits the courts of petty sessions throughout the
island, if some unfortunate client of his who has got
into trouble requires his aid to defend him. On one
occasion a notorious thief was brought up before one
of these local tribunals, charged with stealing a few
shillings' worth of ground provisions. Instead of em-
ploying a lawyer he committed his defence to an
obeah-man, who promised him, in consideration of a
fee of £3, 3s., that on the day of trial he would
attend in court, and by "fixing the eye" of the pre-
siding magistrate, obtain the prisoner's acquittal.
But, all the same, the man was convicted and sentenced to three months' imprisonment, with hard
labour.

Serpent or devil worship is by no means rare in

the country districts; and of its heathen rites the obeah-man is invariably the priest. Many of them keep a stuffed snake in their huts as a domestic god—a practice still common in Africa, from which of course the custom has been derived.[1] One of the commonest deceptions which the obeah-man practises upon his dupes, is by persuading them that they have lost their shadows.[2] "I was present," says Mr. Barclay, "some years ago, at the trial of a notorious obeah-man, driver on an estate in the parish of St. David, who, by the overwhelming influence he had acquired over the minds of his deluded victims, and the more potent means he had at command to accomplish his ends, had done great injury among the slaves on the property before it was discovered. One of the witnesses, a negro belonging to the same estate, was asked—'Do you know the prisoner to be an obeah-man?' '*Ees, massa; shadow-catcher true.*' 'What do you mean by shadow-catcher?' '*Him heb coffin* [a little coffin produced] *him set fo catch dem shadow.*' 'What shadow do you mean?' '*When him set obeah for summary*

[1] "Among the annual festivals is the pilgrimage of the nation of Fida to the great serpent. The people, collected before the house of the serpent, lying upon their faces, worship his supposed divinity, without daring to look upon him."—Prichard, *Natural History of Man*, p. 533. The Fida, besides the great serpent which is adored by the whole nation, have each their particular smaller serpents, which are worshipped as household gods, but are not esteemed so powerful by far as the great one, to whom the smaller serpents are subjected.—Prichard, p. 527.

[2] See case given in Waddell's *West Indies and Central Africa*, p. 138. London, 1863.

(somebody) *him catch dem shadow and dem go dead.'*
And too surely they were soon dead, when he pre-
tended to have caught their shadows, by whatever
means it was effected."[1] The same superstition was
found by Mr. Waddell in full force in Calabar; and
it may assist in enabling us to understand its meaning, when we keep in view that in the language of
that country the word for "shadow" is the same as
that for "soul."[2]

I have before me the records of the slave courts
held for the parish of Portland between the years
1805 and 1816. They are full of cases of Obeah.
One woman attempts to murder her master by putting arsenic into his noyeau; another by mixing
pounded glass with his coffee; a third is charged
with practising upon the credulity of his fellow-slaves
by pretending to cure another of a sore in his leg,
and "taking from thence sundry trifles,—a hawk's
toe, a bit of wire, and a piece of flesh."

On 22d February 1831 William Jones was tried
and sentenced to death "for conspiring and contriv-
ing to destroy William Ogilvie, overseer of Fairy
Hill estate in the parish of Portland." The notes
of the evidence taken at the trial state:—"This pro-
secution arises out of the confession of Thomas
Lindsay, who was shot to death pursuant to the
sentence of a court-martial, on the 31st day of January
1832. The part of the confession which inculpates

[1] Barclay's *Present State of Slavery in the West Indies,* pp.
190-191. London, 1827.
[2] Waddell, p. 139.

William Jones is as follows :—' About three weeks before Christmas me and David Anderson, and William Rainey, and Alexander Simpson being together, the devil took hold of us, tell us we must destroy the overseer; and he agreed to go to a man named William Jones, belonging to Providence Mountain, an obeah-man, to give us something to kill the busha, so that his horse may throw him down and break his neck in a hole. Jones said as this was a great thing he could not do it for less than a doubloon, and we had only five shillings to give him. But we agree to carry him a barrow (a hog) with five dollars, and a three-gallon jug of rum, and three dollars in cash. He then gave us something and told us to give it to the waiting-boy to throw it in the water, and that would kill him. The waiting-boy, James Oliver, did throw it into the water, but it did the busha no harm, and the waiting-boy said the obeah-man was only laughing at us. We then went to the obeah-man, and he said the waiting-boy could not have put the things into the water. And then he came himself one day, took the bag of an ant's house, etc. etc. etc.'" "Here," says the report, "follows an account of obeah tricks practised." It then goes on :—" *David Anderson*, sworn. He [witness] was run away three months before Christmas in consequence of the overseer flogging him for stealing some rum from his brother Henry Simpson and putting water in the place of it. He and four others went to William Jones. William Rainey explained the cause of their coming—that he

OBEAH.

carried one macaroni, and four bitts, and a jug of rum, and that Alexander Simpson carried a pig. The obeah-man (the prisoner) asked a doubloon. He gave them something in a nancy bag pounded up, which James Oliver put into the busha's drink, but it did not do him. That they then fetched the obeah-man down to the estate, where he gave them something to put in the step of the door—all to kill the busha. The prisoner had a cutacoo. They gave him a two-dollar piece, beside the money they had before given.

"*Benny Simpson*, Fairy Hill, sworn—Says the prisoner came into the house of her father, Adam Fisher, where he stayed two weeks, and that he was employed making obeah to kill the busha. She was afraid of the man. Thomas Lindsay, Davy Anderson, and Sammy Taylor brought him there. She was not allowed to go into the house, as he was making obeah to kill the busha. William Rainey showed the guilty parties the pass to find out prisoner. When her daddy, Adam Fisher, heard that James Purrier was taken up, he went away, saying he would destroy himself. He has not been heard of since."

On the 13th April of the same year William Fisher was tried and convicted for pretending to supernatural power. Edward Francis, slave to Fairfield, being "sworn and admonished," said :—"On Wednesday, about the first week in May of last year, I was at my father-in-law's house. This was shortly after Mr. Speed came as overseer to the estate. Tom, *alias* Richard Mein, Richard Passley, the driver of Fairfield, prisoner, and others, came in. Fisher called for a fowl's egg, which he put into a basin. Tom Crowder sat beside him. Fisher threw rum over the egg, and set it on fire, and when the egg was boiled in the rum he broke it, gave it to Tom to suck, who declined. Fisher, after sucking the egg, rubbed part of the shell in his hand until it was mashed. He then put it with some stuff which he said was cinnamon into a phial. It was a thing which he said would turn anybody's mind. He then gave it to me, and said it was to be given to driver Richard, who would give it to the horse-stable-boy, to put under the horse's tail, when the horse would throw the busha, Mr. Speed, down and break his neck. I was obliged to go back to Fair-field to fetch the money before he gave me the phial. He would not trust me without I got the money from Justina. Fisher likewise gave me some of the egg-shell, and [told me] to rub it up and strew it about the yard—that if the stuff in the phial did not make the horse throw the busha, this would. Robert Mein [slave] to Cold Harbour, had a bad leg. Fisher pricked the place, and black blood came. Fisher then sucked the part and spit out two beads. At another time, when I ran away, I met Fisher in the pass, and he took me up to his mountain and gave me a bush to chew, and said if I went home without it I should get fum fum, as the busha was swearing after me very much. I gave him four bits for it. When I went home busha did fum me, and I then went back to Fisher to get the money from him. He said,

'No, there is a different way to manage the busha,' which was to kill him. On the Wednesday night before mentioned, Fisher gave Solomon Passley a little bit of stick, which he told him to chew and spit it all about the pass, and this would kill busha. The whole estate said they would go to somebody to kill the busha. They all agreed to look out for a man for that purpose.

"*By Court.*—What money did you give Fisher for the stuff in the phial?

"Half-a-dollar, which Justina gave me.

"Did you not go to fetch Fisher?

"No; driver Richard sent me to get the stuff. He said in the mill-house that every one must throw up money to kill the busha.

"Did Justina complain to you of your having kept the money and not given it to Fisher?

"She said I had eaten the money, I had not given it to Fisher, as no good had come. Fisher had not killed the busha, and the money was given for so-so.

"What did you do with the phial?

"I carried it and broke it against the horse-stable, and covered it with dirt.

"Was it the intention of the whole estate's people to kill Mr. Speed?

"Yes, we all employed Fisher."

"*Alexander Hartley to Fairfield*, sworn—saith that he knows Fisher. He is a Mungola man. He is a bush man—an obeah man. Heard when runaway, and living in a cave, that money had been thrown up for the purpose of killing Mr. Speed."

The practice of Obeah amongst the humbler classes is still, unfortunately, as prevalent at the present day, despite the severely penal laws against it, as it was in the beginning of the century.

A local paper, *The Gleaner* of 26th January 1869, quoting from *The Falmouth Post*, relates the following story :—

"During the past week the town of Lucea was kept in a state of considerable excitement, in consequence of a report which was circulated and believed, not only by the lower but middling classes, that a Spanish jar, containing a large quantity of gold coins, had been discovered in the yard adjoining the premises of a black man, named Johnson, near to Weir Park settlement, about a mile from the town of Lucea. The report of the discovery was strengthened by the assertion of several persons, male and female, that preparations on an extensive scale, and commensurate with the stated value, were being made for the purpose of taking up the jar and its contents. We instituted an inquiry, and ascertained that many of the friends of the man Johnson were assisting in doing all he suggested,—that obeah-men were employed by the parties immediately concerned,— that the obeah-men were supplied with an abundance of food and liquor,—and that nights were passed in the performance of superstitious rites which disturbed the Christian-minded villagers in the neighbourhood. A white cock was killed on one occasion, for the purpose of carrying out one of the objects that was declared necessary, and there were sacrifices of goats and pigs, the spilling of blood in all directions, and the commission of other abominations, which we have neither time nor inclination to mention.

"On Sunday, 17th instant, the excitement was greater than on preceding days. One of the crowd remarked, that all attempts made to take the jar from the earth would be unavailing, until human blood was sprinkled on the land,—'that human blood must be used, for nothing else would answer.' On hearing this remark, and seeing that hundreds of persons were on their way to the spot, and that the constabulary were proceeding thither for the maintenance of order, we determined upon accompanying them. On arriving in front of Johnson's house, where upwards of 400 men, women and children, were assembled, an inspection was made of the piece of land where the treasure was said to be, and one of the constables, having been engaged a few minutes in turning up the earth, while Johnson and his family were giving utterance to angry expressions, aided by a young man named Langshaw (a clerk in one of the stores in Lucea), who talked about the rights of property, etc., found a clayed cooking utensil, called a yabba, and a common water jar, both of which had been evidently placed in the newly-excavated earth by Johnson and his associates. At the discovery of the imposture, a shout of indignation was raised by some of the assembled people, and between them and Johnson's family there was a violent altercation. Upon a gentleman remarking that the whole affair was a compound of Obeahism,

K

Myalism, and Revivalism, some of the bystanders observed, that if the white people had not interfered the jar and money would have been found. One of the black lookers-on said, 'The jar began to sink down as soon as the white people began to trouble it.' The house of Johnson was afterwards searched by the constabulary, who took from it blocks and ropes that Langshaw had supplied for lifting up the treasure ; and on inquiry being made, the fact was ascertained that Obeahism had been at work for several days and nights. We are informed that three Obeah-men, who were not apprehended at the time we left Lucea, had received £10 for their services, and that for some months past they have had other and well-paying customers in Lucea, some of whom are among the most earnest in professions of Christianity."

The Obeah-man must not be confounded with the Myalman, who is to the former what the antidote is to the poison. He professes to undo what the other has done; to cure where the other has injured ; but it must be confessed that, both in its operation and its results, the cure is often worse than the disease. In truth, the boundary line between the two classes of professors is oftentimes but a shadowy one.

Obeah, apparently, is not destined to die an inglorious death,—*quia caret vate sacro.* In 1817, there was published in London a book, entitled, " Poems, chiefly on the Superstition of Obeah,"—a curious work, on a curious and far from uninteresting subject.

XIV.

FROM Chapelton we proceeded to Mandeville, the principal village—for it is nothing more—of the parish of Manchester, and one of the healthiest stations in the island.

Situated in the heart of the Manchester mountains, and about 2000 feet above the level of the sea, the climate of this pretty little place is almost European in its character. In the winter months, the thermometer has been known to register 55° during the night, and the maximum heat never exceeds 75° or 80°.

The road ascends through park-like scenery, gradually but unintermittently from Porus, a gloomy straggling village about ten miles from Mandeville. Here we first became acquainted with the Manchester "red dirt," as the negroes call it,—a dark ferruginous "brick mould," in composition a mixture of iron and alumina, which persistently covers the whole surface of the parish.

The change of temperature was very marked as we ascended the hill.

It was evening when we passed through Porus,

and we had hardly left it five miles behind us when we were glad to don our greatcoats and wrap ourselves up in travelling rugs.

" The sun never rose upon a more picturesque village than that of Mandeville," says Sewell, who visited it in 1860.[1] " It reminded me a little of a newly located town in an American territory, for the houses did not look very old, nor were the streets out of repair,—two exceptions to very general rules in Jamaica."

To our mind it was more like an English country village. There was a village green where the schoolboys played cricket ; a square-towered white-washed English village church ; a clean little school-house, and one or two pretty cottages, with patches of flowers before their doors. There were pastures divided by stone walls,—a rare sight in this country, and English-like trees in the common, and cows browsing underneath their shade.

Here we pitched our tents for some days, taking up our quarters in one of the cleanest and most comfortable lodging-houses which we came across in Jamaica.

There was a garden too, or rather what had once been a garden, now a tangled wilderness of trees, and shrubs and flowers, many of them rare even for the tropics.

It was pleasant in the morning to look out of your bedroom window and watch the humming-birds flitting about amongst the great trumpet-like flowers

[1] *Ordeal of Free Labour*, p. 222.

of the Portlandia, or the scarlet blossoms of the hibiscus, or the pink clusters of the lilac. Then there were rich orchids which scented the air of nights. There was the Holy Ghost plant, with its pure white petals, shrouding the snowy Dove within.

There was the wax-plant, trailing over the window frames, flower, stem, and leaves, as if cunningly formed in wax. There was the spider orchid, growing upon an old guava tree, and honeysuckle twining over the pillars of the piazza. Jasmines and frangipanis perfumed our sitting-room; and our daily nosegay was formed of stephanotis and heliotrope, of gigantic lilies of exquisite hue and delicate odour, of clove-scented carnations, and Martinique roses.

In the yard were loquat, orange and bread-fruit trees. The ground was carpeted with the magenta blossoms of the Tahiti apple; and a handsome star-apple tree, with quivering leaves, green on the upper, bronze on the lower surface, justified the negro proverb, that "woman deceitful like a 'tar apple leaf."

The peasantry of Manchester are a prosperous, contented, and independent race. Many of them are well off. We were told of one man, who, by industry and frugality, had accumulated £2000. Coffee is the principal staple of the parish. It is calculated that on an average each of the small settlers makes £80 per annum from his coffee crops. But grazing farms are numerous, and Manchester cattle and horses are highly esteemed throughout the island. There can be little poverty in a district where the poorest man owns his patch of land, and rides to market on his own "beast."

Manchester has always been the head-quarters of the Moravian Mission in Jamaica, and to the praise-worthy efforts of the clergy of that denomination is to be attributed much of the improved social position of the peasantry in the parish.

One of our first visits was to the Moravian settlement of Fairfield.

We left Mandeville about twelve o'clock. The morning had been dull and cloudy, with little or no breeze. But towards mid-day a gentle gale sprang up, and shortly afterwards the sun shone forth in unclouded brilliancy. The road for the first few miles was rough and stony. Recent rains had worn it away into deep ruts and spring-breaking holes, and our carriage-wheels were often impeded by the luxuriant growth of grass and "bush" which told of the infrequency of traffic over the solitary highway. But every tree and rock was clothed with verdure. Ipomæas dangled from the boughs of the orange trees. Golden, white, and purple creepers—a mazy thicket of colour—bordered the road like a hedge. The night-blowing cereus, with closed, tassel-like flowers, dragged its fleshy stems over every broken wall and limestone boulder. By degrees the land-scape opened, and through the breaks in the bush we caught glimpses of the far-off sea, misty and hazy in the distance. Then came a village, with one or two decent cottages, and a blue-fronted grog-shop. Then a few huts, with tiny barbacues and green patches of coffee. Then the wooden spire of Fairfield church was seen; and in a few minutes more we had driven up to the door of the resident clergyman's house.

From the little grey verandah, festooned with creepers, into which we were courteously invited to enter, we could command a magnificent view of the surrounding country.

Over against us lay the low range of the Santa Cruz mountains. Through dips in the sky-line to the right and left of the landscape, we looked down upon the sea at Black River and Alligator Pond. Below us, at the foot of Spur Tree Hill, was a wide and extensive valley, stretching out like yellow downs when it trended away to the sea, in other parts green with bright pastures, or black with dark masses of foliage.

The settlement of Fairfield includes a church, infant, training, and day school. The community possess about forty-eight acres of land, of which twelve are in cultivation. The number of communicants upon the roll is about a thousand. The average attendance of scholars at the day school is over forty, and at the infant school about thirty-five. Boys and girls here receive a sound liberal and Christian education. The girls are, in addition, taught sewing, cookery, and housekeeping. The boys are brought up to trades or educated as teachers.

We first visited the day school, where the boys were busy with their copy books. A large blue globe, made from the pith of the dagger plant (*Yucca aloifolia*, Adam's needle), by a former "brother," hung on a framework from the roof of the room. Close beside it stood the teacher's desk. A shelving platform with benches for the boys, a clock, a black board on an easel, a map of Jamaica, and a drawing of a sugar manufactory, completed the furniture of the apartment. Music is energetically cultivated amongst the pupils, and with surprisingly good results, considering the unworkable materials the teachers have to deal with. For the negroes, impressionable as they are to the influence of music, are the least musical creatures in creation. A negress's voice is shriller than the most strident fife ; a negro's is harsh and wooden. Time and harmony are beyond the comprehension of either. A hymn sung by a negro congregation is a race, where the object of every one is either to distinguish himself by some eccentric performance of his own on the way, or to reach the goal, the end of the verse, before his neighbours. But at Fairfield the boys sang some hymns and part songs with wonderful effect, and much credit is due to the earnest, fair-headed German, who laboured assiduously at this most thankless of tasks.

In the infant school, which we next visited, knots of tiny children, under the charge of monitors often smaller than their pupils, were picking out their letters, or spelling words of one syllable. Here, as in the day school, we were struck with the excellent system which prevailed. Talent was everywhere encouraged; the brightest and cleverest children being selected to instruct the more backward, entirely irrespective of age.

The training-school boasts an excellent garden, neatly and trimly kept by the labour of the students themselves. The church now in the course of erection is a handsome stone building, commanding an exquisite view over sea and valley. And in the pastures attached to it are some most curious fig-trees, evidently of great age, whose roots have wound themselves round and over and in and out the crevices of the limestone boulders.

The very peculiar manner in which social requirements are combined with religious duties in the doctrine and practice of the Moravian Church of necessity requires a special training for the young members of both sexes of that denomination. The teachers and clergy belonging to the Moravian body have wives selected for them by lot, and for this purpose a training-school for young women has been established at Bethabara near Newport, a little village some ten or fifteen miles from Fairfield. Here, in addition to the sound religious education which they receive, they are taught house-keeping, cookery, and other domestic duties. Before a clergyman can be inducted into a cure he is bound to marry, and if he loses his wife during his incumbency, he is either suspended from discharging his priestly duties, or is removed to some other sphere of usefulness.

By virtue of her marriage, his wife acquires a certain sacerdotal character. Clothed like her husband, and also like the communicants, in white, she administers the sacrament to the females, whilst her husband does the like to the males. She is in theory the mother, and her husband the father, of their flock. No member of the Moravian Church is entitled to go to law until he has received the sanction of his minister, a privilege accorded only after attempts at an amicable arrangement of the dispute have failed, or in special cases of grievous wrong, reparable in no other way.

Our drive home was by Spur-tree and Bulldead. We mention these places only as instances of the quaint names which villages and houses in Jamaica obtain. Looking over a list of properties in an old almanac, I found amongst the estates such names as Paradise, Angels, Thrive-well, Heart's-ease, Hog-hole, Lilliput, Pumpkin-ground, Mount-prosperous, Cow Park, Trial, Boggetty Hill, Pleasant Hall, Snaky Hill, Envy Hall, Scholar's Cot, Mount Moses, Poor Man's Corner, Brumalia, Apropos, Done-at-last, Hobson's Choice, Try-see, Grumble Hall, Shot-over, Come-see, Iter Boreale, Puckle-church, Fat-hog-Quarter, Save-rent, Slippery Gut, Millennium Hall, Running Gut, Purling Stream, Shoes and Stockings, and Y. S. A stream in Manchester goes by the name of the One-stick-over-the-one-eye River. A well-known village in the Maroon was called " Me no sen', you no come." At the present day every negro settlement is either a Comfort or a Content, a Friendship or a Providence, a Prospect or a Retirement. Happy Huts, Pleasant Groves, Cheerful Gardens, Harmony Penns, Golden Vales, Fruitful Mounts, Unity Valleys, and Cherry Banks, abound; and the more wild and desolate the situation, the more jocund and cheery its name.

XV.

THE ST. ELIZABETH PLAINS.

THE Creoles have a prejudice, which they do not attempt to explain, against travelling by night. But immediately after second cock-crow[1] is no uncommon hour for starting, especially when the day's journey is likely to be a long one. Once or twice we were fain to adopt this practice, and it must be confessed that the extra exertion which it involved brought with it its own reward.

The cool, often chilly, morning air, the deserted roads, the calm and quiet of surrounding nature —with "the full fair moon" shining overhead, and the harmless lightning playing around—had all an indescribable charm of their own. And the many romantic scenes through which these morning drives led me have left an impression upon my mind which will not readily be effaced. Now the road wound through a wild savanna—prolific in naught but wire-grass—its wide desert-like expanse broken only by a few stunted guava bushes; now we were passing a negro village half hidden by the dense

[1] The negroes say that cocks crow thrice during the night—at 10 p.m. ; 1 a.m. ; and 4 a.m.

growth of brushwood around it; now travelling under an avenue of magnificent trees, through whose leafy roof the moonbeams in vain struggled for admittance. The graceful and varied character of the foliage cannot fail to be remarked by all travellers in the tropics. The feathery tufts of the bamboo, the dotted outline of the logwood, the coral-like branches of the calabash, the large palmate leaf of the bread-fruit, and the glossy arc-like arms of the cocoa-nut palm, never appeared to me so beautiful as when seen *en profile* against the morning sky, or when forming part of the walls of such an avenue as that which I have described.

But nothing struck me so much in these morning journeys as the extraordinary stillness that seemed to fall upon all nature just before dawn. Not a sound was to be heard except the monotonous tramp of your horse's feet. The shrill song of the grasshopper, the quick sharp chirp of the cricket, and the hoarse croaking of the bull-frog,—all had ceased.

By degrees the day began to break. First, a faint brightness was seen in the eastern sky; then a flush of rosy light dawned on the landscape. The dark blue-black night-clouds sank down in heavy masses below the horizon. The moon paled—one solitary star retaining its brilliancy long after its neighbours had disappeared. A gentle twittering of birds was heard; a white screech-owl flew shrieking across the path; and then uprose the glorious sun, and it was day once more.

Such an early start as that which I have described

we made on the day that we left Mandeville for the parish of St. Elizabeth's. And here we may in passing state that a parish in Jamaica is of the nature of a county in England. It has its separate commission of the peace, its *custos rotulorum*, clerk of petty session, clerk of the parish board, collector of taxes, clerk of the parochial road board, coroner and rector; and a circuit court is held in its principal town or village. The whole island is divided into fourteen parishes not very unequal in population, and, with the exception of the city and parish of Kingston, not very unequal in area.[1] The parish of St. Elizabeth's, with which we are now about to make aquaintance, has an area of 448 square miles, and had, in 1864, a population of 37,777 souls.

By the time that

> " Phœbus had sprung free Thetis' lap,
>   The hills with rays adorning,"

we were well-nigh at the top of Watson's hill, one of those steep inclines—it can hardly be called a road —made for descent rather than for ascent, by which the inhabitants of the mountain regions gain access to the plains below.

We could detect a marked difference in the character of the surrounding vegetation. The little Palmetto palm, with which the negroes thatch their houses, and whose leaves the negresses use as umbrellas on their journeys, was common. So also was the Mountain Cabbage (*Areca oleracea*), waving its

[1] Governor Grant's *Report on the State of the Colony, for* 1867. 24th October 1868.

graceful form, like a tall Corinthian pillar, often 150 feet high above the encircling foliage. Its *pith*, as it is popularly called, *chou de palmiste*, as the French term it, is perhaps the most delicate vegetable in the tropics. In a country where oysters grow on trees, and crabs burrow in the woods, we need not be surprised to hear that cabbages are cut with an axe. Such is the case with the Areca. The taking of the cabbage, as with all the palm tribe, kills the tree. The roads were bordered with a flower-fence of Barbadoes pride (*Poinciana pulcherrima*), or in negro idiom, "doodle-doo;" and over its pea-covered stems twined the liquorice vine (*Abrus precatorius*), whose scarlet and black spotted seeds ("John Crow or Jumby beads") are well known in this country as necklaces. There, too, trailed the Circassian bean (*Adenanthera Pavonina*), whose seeds are said to be so constantly uniform in weight, that jewellers in the East Indies employ them as weights; and the Jerusalem thorn, which is popularly supposed to be the plant with which our Saviour was crowned.

On reaching the level we passed Littets', a Moravian station, with a good church, as all these settlements have. The road here was very uninteresting for a mile or two. The soil was dry and sandy. Great quantities of a kind of willow covered the plains, and at rare intervals a seaside grape-tree or two (*Coccoloba uvifera*), whose wood is admirably suited for wood-engraving, and whose fruit makes excellent tarts.

It was too early in the morning to see many signs

of life. Once we passed a cart with the motto
"Trust to God, my friend!" painted in bright letters
on its sides, driven by

> " A somewhat pottle-bodied boy,"

and carrying in it an aged woman, like the negro's
pig, " little, but very old." Then a party of Coolies
came tramping by, the women bedecked with orna-
ments, with gold pins stuck in their noses, and, in
the upper lobes of their ears, ear-rings so heavy that
the ear was pulled down by their weight, rings on
their fingers, necklaces round their thick dusky
throats, half-a-dozen bracelets on each arm, and
bangles round each arm ankle.

A little above Littets', we commenced the ascent
of the Santa Cruz hills. For the next ten miles the
journey was a constant ascent. The roads were for-
tunately capital, and the views of the sea, from various points, exquisite. From Torrington we could
look down over all the St. Elizabeth plains, and far
away in the distance, covered with a sunny haze,
stretched the green cane-pieces and fertile fields of
verdant Westmoreland.

At the little village of Malvern, we passed a shoemaker's shed, from whose sign-board we copied the
following inscription :

> " I'm a maker of boots and shoes,
> No man's work will I refuse,
> My work is good, my price is just :
> Excuse me, my friend, I cannot trust."

Here we stopped for breakfast, and were introduced for the first time to the famous Avocado or

Alligator pear (*Persea gratissima*). This celebrated vegetable is the correct accompaniment of " 'pose-upon "* (as the negroes call salt fish), and is an excellent substitute for fresh butter. The story is told of an irascible old planter, who nearly dismissed a book-keeper upon his estate for eating butter at breakfast, during the pear season : " for a man who can do that," he growled out, "upon the wages I give him, cannot possibly be honest." The Alligator pear is also eaten as a fruit, mixed with sugar and wine. The seeds contain a large quantity of tannin. A cloth stretched over them and pricked with a pin may be marked as indelibly as with the best marking ink.

Resuming our journey in the cool of the evening, we left the buggy to follow, and rode down to the foot of the hill. Mango trees of all kinds, laden with fruit, became common—from the humble " turpentine " to the proud " No. 11." The " sea-loving cocoa-nut " waved its quivering leaves, and by its crooked, wind-bent stems, illustrated the negro saying, " as uncommon as a straight cocoa-nut." St. Elizabeth, as a parish, is famous for its mangoes and its palms. Manchester, on the other hand, has little to boast of, except its coffee and its oranges.

As we were driving along the sea-shore, just before entering the bustling little town of Black

---

[1] "Pose-upon " means "impose upon," and salt fish is a universal stand-by in Jamaica. With these facts before him, we leave the reader to ferret out the signification of this quaint expression for himself.

L

River, we met one of the old-fashioned "kittereens," a vehicle once universal in Jamaica, and still known, we believe, in some outlandish districts in Cornwall. It was a queer, high-bodied gig, with an umbrella fixed on the top of a pole by way of a hood. There was little protection from the sun in a covering of that description.

As we were wondering at this old-world turn-out, the nut of a sand-bag tree, expanded with the heat, burst with a loud explosion.

"Warra!" cried Bob, nearly jumping from his driving box, "what for debbil shoot pistol to kill poor nigger so?"

The rest of our day's "travel" was accomplished without either accident or incident. We drove into Black River when the sun was setting, and here we remained for the night. The wharf was crowded with logwood, out of which the Jew speculators of the enterprising little place were just then making enormous fortunes.

As we were smoking our after-dinner cigars, leaning over the old wooden bridge which here spans the Black River, we saw a dull, black mass sailing slowly up stream. It was, as we suspected, an alligator. Forthwith the Creole friend who accompanied us launched out into "alligator stories," which had at least the merit of being horrible, to render them interesting in our eyes. He told us how one day an alligator carried off the calf of a poor woman, which was browsing peaceably by the side of its mother. The woman called for assistance, and succeeded in bringing an old fisherman, who was hauling in his lines at some little distance, to her help. When the man came up he found the cow busily engaged in butting the alligator. Cutting a stiff bamboo pole, the man rushed to the rescue, and succeeded in killing the alligator by shoving the pole down its throat. On another occasion an alligator attacked a woman who was crossing the sands on horseback, and tore out the horse's entrails. But such occurrences are rare. The alligator is fully more frightened for the human race than they need be for it.

Jamaica possesses nearly a hundred rivers, but of these only two are navigable, the Black River, in St. Elizabeth's, and the Cabarita, in Westmoreland. "On these streams flat-bottomed boats and canoes bring produce from the upper plains to the sea. The other rivers subserve the purposes of mill economy, but are rarely rendered available for irrigation." [1]

The whole parish of St. Elizabeth's, with the single exception of that portion of it which embraces the Santa Cruz mountains, is one dead level, broken up by lagoons and marshes when it approaches the sea, but singularly devoid of streams. Indeed, but for the slow-flowing streams of the Black River, it might be described as waterless. Tank water is therefore largely employed for domestic purposes.

The prevalence of extensive plains on the south side of the island, and the short course of the rivers on the north side, has been often noticed.

[1] Transactions of the Jamaica Royal Society of Arts, 1855, p. 27.

In the level "downs" of St. Elizabeth, life is less rapid, less intense than in more hilly regions. Nature is not dead, but asleep. The rivers flow with less rapid pace; the breezes blow with less reviving energy; the heat is greater; the vegetation less varied; even the birds of the air sweep over the tract of heaven with dull and hebetate wing.

In the great savanna of St. Elizabeth's resides a curious colony of blacks whose origin has puzzled most travellers. They go by the name of Paratees, and build their huts in the little clumps of bush with which the plain is dotted. They have no religion, no tradition; they are extremely shy, and shun the society of, or even intercourse with, white men. From their long coarse hair, their narrow almond-shaped eyes (not round and bull-eyed, like those of the negroes), and thin well-chiselled, though broad-lobed noses, it is supposed that they are of Indian origin. Parchment is a common name amongst them, —a word which contains the prefix Para, which is also found in Paratee. Although they marry out of their own tribe, such marriages are not liked amongst them. They form a curious and by no means uninteresting problem to the ethnologist.

Black River has the reputation of being one of the most unhealthy towns in Jamaica. The heat is intense, and I shall not readily forget the wretched night I spent there, in a curtainless bed, eaten up by mosquitoes, and maddened almost to fever pitch by the monotonous break of the sea upon the sandy beach. I was suffering from chigoes, too, a little flea which burrows beneath the flesh of your foot, causing you infinite irritation. One felt he could appreciate, to its fullest extent, Sydney Smith's account of the insect miseries of tropical countries : —" Insects are the curse of tropical climates. The *bête rouge* lays the foundation of a tremendous ulcer. In a moment you are covered with ticks. Chigoes bury themselves in your flesh, and hatch a large colony of young chigoes in a few hours. They will not live together; but every chigoe sets up a separate ulcer, and has his own private portion of pus. Flies get entry into your mouth, into your eyes, into your nose; you eat flies, drink flies, and breathe flies. Lizards, cockroaches, and snakes get into your bed; ants eat up the books; scorpions sting you on the foot. Everything bites, stings, or bruises. Every second of your existence you are wounded by some piece of animal life, that nobody has ever seen before but Swammerdam or Meriam. An insect with eleven legs is swimming in your tea-cup; a nondescript with nine wings is struggling in the small beer; or a caterpillar, with several dozen eyes in his belly, is hastening over the bread and butter! All nature is alive, and seems to be getting all her entomological host to eat you up as you are standing, out of your coat, waistcoat, and breeches! Such are the tropics! All this reconciles us to our dens, bogs, vapours, and drizzle; to our apothecaries rushing about with gargle and tincture; to our old British constitutional coughs, sore throats, and swelled faces."

XVI.

IN BLUEFIELDS BAY.

OUR next " station " was the little fishing hamlet
of Bluefields, in the parish of Westmoreland, on the
bay of the same name, once an old Spanish station
by the name of Oristana, at the Buff[1] or Great
House of which Gosse resided while studying the
natural history of the island.

Here we spent some days, occupying the cool of
the mornings and of the evenings in exploring the
neighbourhood and becoming acquainted with its
local peculiarities.   One of these was a negro village
called New Broughton, whose houses were built on
stakes some three or five feet from the ground.
Another was the verdant pastures of Guinea-grass[2]
with which the whole parish abounds.   Few more
refreshing sights greet the traveller's eye in his journeys throughout the island than a bright field of

---

[1] Buff, contraction for "above."   The Great House or Mansion
house of an estate is generally situated on a little hill; hence the
name.

[2] Guinea-grass was introduced into Jamaica in 1744.   The seed
came as food for some birds sent from Africa as a present to the
then Chief Justice.   The birds dying, the seed was thrown away.
— *West India Sketch Book*, vol. ii. p. 9.   London, 1834.

this valuable grass, often five or six feet high, with the passing sea breeze sweeping over it like a wave, and bending its lofty stems with gentle undulatory motion.

A third of the local peculiarities of this district was the number and variety of birds we fell in with. Flocks of green parrots and yellow canaries flew over our heads. Little ground doves, quails, and partridges hopped across the path. The red-throated woodpecker crept· up the high trees. Black and golden banana birds, two-penny chicks, and mocking-birds, flitted out and into the mysterious recesses of the bush. The old-man bird, with its long tail and slow solemn flight, every now and then appeared from out the branches of the cedar trees. The Barbadoes blackbird, with its white glassy eye, occupied its leisure hours in picking the ticks from the backs of the cattle feeding on the pasture. Pouch-billed pelicans swept over the blue bay. Boobies sat in wise conclave on the rock-ledges of " the caves."

In the early morning the swallows and martens flew shrieking over the roof of the house. During the day the little picaflors (humming-birds) with hurried "twittering" flight fluttered round the scarlet blossoms of the shoeblack (*Hibiscus*) ; and of nights, when the sun was down and the thick dew was falling, a weird old owl flew out of her nest on the high cotton-tree, and roamed hither and thither over the pasture in search of food for her screaming progeny.

At dinner time, too, we could always reckon upon

a plentiful game course. Bald-pates, white-wings, and pea-doves were never wanting. Duck and teal came to us from the neighbouring ponds; the Jamaica ortolan (*Motacilla*) from the pastures; and once or twice a stray negro from Maroon land, across the verdure-covered hills to the back of the house, brought us a wild Guinea-fowl or a ring-tail pigeon, of all game in Jamaica the most delicate and the most prized. The larger birds we generally shot ourselves; for the smaller ones we were indebted to the little negro boys who caught them in springs called " calabans," baited with peas or pulse.

Underneath our house was a burn of crystal water, in which every evening our negro servant set his fish-pot for cray-fish and mountain mullet. His " pot " was a bamboo basket with a hole to admit of the entrance of the fish; and the bait was a Seville orange cut in two. Each morning when he went " to search it " he brought back with him, besides his piscatory spoil,

"A cheap and wholesome salad from the brook,"

in the shape of water-cresses, which in the exhausting heat were most grateful.

What recked it though we got beef but once a week, and mutton only when some neighbouring proprietor chose to sacrifice a sheep, if we could feast on hicatee (land-turtle) and black crab, and fare sumptuously every day on *bisque à l'écrivisse* and turtle-fin? To wash down all these delicacies we had penn punch, which seemed to consist mainly of brandy and cherry brandy, main sheet, sangaree,

man dram, and a host of " beverages " of which not
the least acceptable was sweetened lime-juice and
water, with just a soupçon of nutmeg and perhaps
a teaspoonful of old rum to qualify the whole. Truly
we rose from every meal with grateful hearts and
could with unction repeat the negro grace,

" Tank you, me fader, fe all me na swallow,
Hope me may lib, fe nyam smo' (to eat some more)
to-marrow."

One fine afternoon we paid a visit to an old
worker in tortoise-shell, who lived about half a mile
from the hamlet. He was a respectable mulatto man
with silvery hair and whiskers, and an exceedingly
sweet expression of countenance. He kept a little
roadside store ; but beyond a couple of dozen bottles
of beer and a box of country cigars, his stock-in-trade
seemed none of the largest. One side of his tiny
cottage was hung round with saws and files of all
sorts and sizes—the instruments of his craft. He
was suffering from inflammation of the eye, caused by
the dust raised in working the shell. He told us
that of all the fine species of sea-turtle known in
Jamaica, the hawk's-bill turtle was the only one
whose shell was of any value. A single shell would
weigh about four or five pounds, and was sold from
eight to ten shillings a pound. The fisher people
shell the turtle after death by laying it on its back
over a hot fire, when it scales off. The Spaniards of
the Main, more cruel, not unfrequently shell it whilst
still living and then let it go. Dark thick tortoise-
shell is esteemed the best. The mode of working it

is to wash it over with water and ashes, and then polish it with charcoal and olive oil. It can then be moulded to any form by the action of heat.

We subsequently visited a turtle "crawl" in Sheffield Bay. It was a little fenced-in enclosure underneath some mangrove trees. Four green turtles were swimming about, preparatory to being sold to the trading-vessels at the neighbouring town of Savanna-la-Mar. The usual price is from threepence to fourpence a pound. In very plentiful seasons it sometimes goes down to twopence. "From the time the turtle is deposited on board the vessel conveying it from Jamaica to the day it reaches England, it receives no food whatever. In sailing vessels this starvation continues for seven weeks; in steamers probably only nineteen days. In many vessels the poor turtles lie upon their backs the entire voyage, with nothing but a wet swab under their heads, it being the business of the ship's loblolly boy to wipe from their frothy mouths the accumulation of mucus that clots around them (as thrown off from their diseased lungs), and to clean away from their glassy eyes that deposit of slimy film which would otherwise become a concrete mass, and blind this barbarously treated delicacy for the banquets of the wealthy. So fraught with loss of life is this abominable treatment that it is no unfrequent occurrence for a sailing vessel taking in fifty head of turtle to lose thirty or forty on the homeward passage. By steamer (seldom carrying more than twenty-five head) the percentage of death is little in comparison   but the barbarity of prolonged starvation is the same, only less intensified by the difference between the length of voyage."[1]

Of the various species of turtle which are known in Jamaica,—the green turtle, the hawk's-bill, the mulatto or yellow turtle, the trunk, and the Macongo, the green is the only kind sold as food. The inferior sorts are eaten by the fisher-folk alone. It is, besides, the largest. The average weight of a full-grown green turtle is about 400 lbs. There was a Macongo turtle caught at Negril in 1843, which weighed a ton, produced a whole barrel of oil, and took nine men to turn over. "A turtle does not reach its true perfection of flavour, its growth of fat, its development of gelatine, its mature proportion of calipee, its breadth of calipash, its unctuosity of fins, its true piquancy of richness and '*noblesse de gout*' until it has achieved the weight of 230 lbs., or over."[2] But as regards the fish sent home to this country, "no captain will purchase a turtle weighing over 120 lbs., as no mature fish would stand the starvational treatment"[2] which we have detailed. As an article of diet turtle is in high repute all over the West Indies. Turtle steak, turtle fins stewed, turtle liver, turtle tripe, and above all turtle eggs, are delicacies which it is almost worth while taking a voyage to Jamaica to procure.

The turtle, for all its apparent apathy, is one of the most cunning of fish, and to capture him requires all the fisherman's skill. When his "lair" has once

[1] *Handbook of the Kingston Preserved Turtle Company*, p. 9. By S. Levien. [2] *Ibid.* p. 10.

been discovered, the fisherman watches his opportunity, and when the turtle is absent in search of
food spreads a square net over the spot.   As soon as
the turtle returns the net is pulled up.   But often a
fish will dodge his hunter for months.   An old boatman told me of one that had taken him ten years to
catch !

Despite the burning, sickening heat of the day,
and the violent " norths " which seemed to shake our
cottage to pieces at night, our stay at Bluefields was
of a very enjoyable nature.   Often in the cool tropical evenings, with their dove-coloured " quaker" skies,
we would go orchid-hunting amongst the mangrove
trees on the shore, wandering over the white sandy
beach covered with pieces of sponge and fragments
of broken coral for hours together.   Often, too, would
we go canoeing in the bay, learning from our coloured
boatman all about the various " schools" of fish which
haunted the bay, and picking up much quaint infor-
mation about the habits and customs and superstitions of the fisher-folk.   Our canoe (the Indian
piragua) was about eleven feet long, and was made
as usual out of a single cotton tree.   Closely packed
—two on each bench—sixteen or seventeen persons
could be accommodated in it.   It could carry from
seventeen to eighteen hundredweight of goods : and
with proper care would last ten years.   Our head-
boatman boasted of it as the safest kind of boat in
the world, and said he could bring a canoe safe to
land in the stormiest weather.

The fishing season lasts from June to September ;

the deep-sea fishing from March to May. The ordinary methods of fishing are with the line and with the seine net. A seine with its two accompanying canoes costs about £50.

Another mode of fishing is with the " palenka." This is " a line of almost interminable length, with any number of hooks affixed to it by other small lines. A common number is three. The largest has 550 hooks on it, at $2\frac{3}{4}$ yards apart, which gives nearly a mile in length of fishing line. By a most ingenious arrangement of a cork pad all round a large basket, each hook is inserted in rotation into it, while the line to which each hook is joined is coiled in the basket itself. As each hook is cast into the sea it is baited with pieces of fish, and then the three lines being joined—fancy the labour of paying out three miles of fishing line, with 1650 hooks at $2\frac{3}{4}$ yard intervals —the end of the line being fixed to heavy stakes driven into the sea bottom, and the whereabout of the stakes only discoverable in the dark and deep of the night by the spring alarm-bells affixed to them. At times the catches are very remunerative, varying with palenkas of the quantity of hooks stated, from four to fourteen dollars. At times not even a dollar's worth is caught."[1] " Ebry day," says the negro proverb, "fishing day, but ebry day no fe catch fish."

Still yet another mode of fishing is with the " bateau," an open kind of punt made of branches of trees loosely nailed together, in which the fisher squats, dropping his line over the bows of his uncouth skiff.

[1] *County Union* newspaper, November 19, 1870.

and with the aid of a paddle no bigger than a cricket bat shifting his position from place to place.

Hand nets are sometimes used for shore fishing. The fisherman wades in up to his neck, then with a dexterous twist above his head casts his net, standing motionless in the water till he thinks it is filled.

Of all the strange creatures that swim the Caribbean Sea perhaps the strangest is the Manatee or Sea-Cow, or as the negroes call it the Mananty. They are very common in these parts. Upwards of thirteen had been seen within the last two years between Black River and Savanna-la-Mar. Popular tradition derives its name from certain fins or flappers near the throat resembling hands. It has a head like an ox, a thick bull-like neck, and a body like a seal; and specimens have been caught from ten to fifteen feet long. It is a timid gentle animal, frightened at the slightest noise and endowed with a remarkably quick sense of hearing. The negroes believe that if you once manage to get up to it, it will allow you to strike its back! It is caught either in the seine or with the harpoon when asleep. It has a little piece of very fine ivory in each ear which is often stolen by the fishermen; and its bones are used to make knife-handles. The flesh is delicious, in some parts resembling pork, in others beef. A spendid "round of beef" can be cut from under the belly.

Another monster of the deep is the sea-devil, which frequently weighs a ton; and the sea-pike, the fiercest fish that swims, which possesses a dorsal fin, which when attacked it raises up, inflicting a heavy backhanded blow. ··

The Sucking-Fish (Remora) is often caught but is not eaten. It is only "cured," that is, dried in the sun, and kept as a curiosity. In the early days of the Spanish conquest, the remora used to be employed by the Indians of Jamaica as falconers employ hawks. It was regularly kept, fed and tamed for the purpose. "The owner on a calm morning carried it out to sea, secured to his canoe by a small but strong line many fathoms in depth. The moment the remora saw a fish in the water, though at a great distance, it started away with the swiftness of an arrow and fastened upon it. The Indian, in the meantime, let go the line which was provided with a buoy that kept on the surface of the sea, and served to mark the course which the fish had taken. This course the Indian pursued in his canoe, until he conceived that his game was nearly exhausted. Then taking up the buoy, he gradually drew the line towards the shore; the remora still adhering to its prey with inflexible tenacity. "By this method," says Ovedo, 'I have known a turtle caught of bulk and weight that no single man could support.'" [1]

Much more quaint lore about the king-fish and the Barracouta, the amber-jack and the horse-eye Carvallhy, the grouper, the black snapper, the old wife, the mud-fish and the parrot-fish, did we glean from our negro boatmen. Many a wild song, such as

> "O my merry Cadoosa,
> What for, you lub man so?"

[1] Dallas's *History of the Maroons*, vol. i. p. 84.

did they sing for our delectation. And when we dismissed them with a little extra largesse "to sweeten their mouths," to use their own phrase, their gratitude and *bouquet d'Afrique* were both alike overpowering.

The drive between Bluefields and Savanna-la-Mar, the chief town of Westmoreland, was, at least for the first half the way, exceedingly beautiful. We passed two or three picturesque little fishing villages, burrowing under over-hanging cliffs, or buried under broad-leaved plantains and bananas. From the honeycombed rocks by the seashore hung long withes with flat glossy leaves. In the yard of one of the negro huts we noticed a large Jaca-tree (*Artocarpus integrifolia*) whose strange noduled fruit, which weighs sometimes sixty or seventy pounds, grows out of its stem. Close by, twining round a cotton tree, whose sap and substance it had utterly destroyed, was a wild fig (*Ficus Indica*); a state of things which in Jamaica is taken as a type of "the Scotchman hugging the Creole to death." Near by it, depended a lovely creeper with brown velvety pods, whose tempting clusters we were about to pluck, when we were suddenly arrested by a loud exclamation from Bob.

"Cracious!" cried he, "if you touch dis ting, I don't know what I will have to do with you. I will hab to get hot hashes" (he meant ashes) "an' put you into dem."

It was the Cow-itch, a plant well known in the pharmacopœia of the old brown women of Jamaica as an electuary, the silky *setæ* of whose pods produce an irritation which covers the body with fearful ulcers and sores.

A little further on we met a child carrying a long bamboo on her head, filled with water from a neighbouring stream—a plan which Bob pronounced to be superior to all the buckets and calibashes in the colony, and which he described as being "as easy as kiss my hand."

At Savanna-la-Mar we were delayed some little time to have certain repairs done to buggy. Our indefatigable Bob proved himself of great service on the occasion, driving in bolts, screwing up nuts and actually painting our broken wheel, as if he were to the manner born.

"Why, Bob!" we said, "we never knew you were so good a painter!"

"Me can't paint!" he exclaimed in a tone of indignant surprise. "Me can't paint! After my grandmother's husban' was a painter, me can't paint!"

This, of course, was conclusive, at least in his eyes. We have already alluded to our "sable and sensuous Sambo's" partiality for dress. Whilst here an incident occurred which amusingly illustrated his predilection for "talky-talky" boots. His shoes having, unlike the Israelites', worn out in his travels, he contracted with a shoemaker in the town to make another pair. But alas! when they were sent home he found that the faithless tradesman had omitted to put "criers" into them, although he had paid him

M

half-a-crown extra for this luxury; and it was with
the greatest difficulty that we could retain him from
taking out proceedings against him under a local
statute called the Tradesman's Act.   He wrote him
a letter however, demanding repayment of the two
and sixpence; and as a specimen of a negro dunning
epistle we now give our readers the benefit of its
perusal.

" SAV.-LE-MAR.

Ap rile the 18, 1871.

" MR. READ, SIR,—I wich to know if you is not in
tend to pay me that small amount.   I will like to
know from you for I think you will have to pay it
befor the Mejistrat.   I am you Bob ——."

From this point we made our way slowly round
the island, returning to Kingston in time to avoid
the May " seasons," ominous symptoms of which had
already begun to shew themselves.   And from thence
one fine morning in spring, as beautiful as that on
which we had first seen " the Queen of the Antilles,"
we embarked for England, carrying with us none but
pleasant recollections of our sojourn in Jamaica.

APPENDIX.

NEGRO PROVERBS.

ALLIGATOR lay egg, but him no fowl.

Ants follow fat.

Bad family better dan empty pigstye.

Before dog go widout him supper, him eat cockroach.

Beggar beg from beggar neber get rich.

Behind dog it is "dog;" behind dog it is "mister dog."

Better belly fe (to) bust dan good ting fe spoil.

Better fe fowl say "dog dead," dan fe dog say "fowl dead."

Big blanket make man sleep late.

Black dog (a small coin) buy trouble, hundred poun' no
    clear him.

Bragging ribber neber drown somebody (anybody).

Brown man's wife eat cockroach in a corner.

Buckra work neber done.

Bull horn neber too heavy for him head.

Cane no grow like grass.

Cashew neber bear guava.

Cedarboard laugh after dead man. (In Jamaica coffins are
    always made of the boards of the cedar-tree.)

Cock mout' (mouth) kill cock.

Cockroach neber in de right before fowl. (An allusion to
    fowls' habit of eating cockroaches.)

Cockroach eber so drunk, him no walk past fowl-yard.

"Come, see me" is nuting; but, "come, lib wi' me" is someting.

Cornful (scornful) dog nyam (eats) dutty [dirty] pudding.

Cotton-tree neber so big but lily (little) axe cut him.

"Cousin Fowl" boil good soup.

Coward man keep whole bones.

Crooked pass (road) hard fe find.

Cry-cry (crying) pickny (child) neber hab him right.

Cubbitch (covetous) for one plum, you lose de whole bunch.

Cuss-cuss (calling names) no bore hole in my skin.

Cuss-cuss no kill John Crow.

Cutacoo (wallet) on man back no yerry (hear) what him massa yerry.

Cunny (cunning) better dan 'trong (strength).

Dead (death) better dan punish (punishment).

De rope you pulling no de one I cutting.

De tune you playing no de one I dancing.

Do fe do (tit for tat) no harm.

Do fe do make Guinea nigger come a' Jamaica.

Dog no eat dog.

Dog say, sooner dan buy nankeen fe sixpence him would give doubloon fe bone.

Duppy (ghost) know who him frighten.

Ebry day da fishing day, but ebry day no fe catch fish.

Ebry dog know him dinner time.

Ebry haul of de net no catch June fish.

Ebry victual fe eat, no ebry story fe talk.

Fat don't feel.

Finger neber say, "Look here;" him say, "Look dere."

Fisherman neber say him fish 'tink (stink).

Follow fashion break monkey neck.

Fowl neber lick (beat) him own chicken too hot.

Full belly tell hungry belly "Take heart!"

Goat say, him hab wool ; sheep say, him hab hair.

Good friend better dan money in de pocket.

Good me do, tank you me get. (This is bitter negro irony.)

Goramighty no lub ugly.

Greedy (greed) choke puppy.

Greedy puppy neber fat.

Hab money, hab friend.

Hand da bowl, knife da troat (throat).

Hand full, hand come.

Hard-eye (wilful) pickny neber go good.

Hog run for him life ; dog run for him character.

Hot needle burn thread.

Hungry belly an' belly full no travel same pass (road).

Hungry fowl wake soon.

Hungry (hunger) make monkey blow fire.

If any one hate you, him gib you basket fe carry water,
   but if you cleber (clever) you put plantain leaf in him (it).

If foot miss pass (the road), him can find him, if mout' miss
   pass him no can find him.

If Mr. Go-'way no come, Mr. Dead will come.

If you see a fippence, you know how dollar is made.

If you want fe lick ole woman pot, you scratch him back.

John Crow neber make house till rain come.

John Crow tink him own pickny white.

John Crow say him de dandy man when him hab so-so
   fedder (feathers).

Left man cocoa (a man's leavings) stick to your belly rib.

Lie worse dan sore.

Lily (little) crab-hole spoil big race horse.

Lily water kill big fire.

Lizard neber plant corn, but him hab plenty.

Man can't smoke an' whistle one time.

Man eber so hearty, dead day watch him.

Man help tief (thief) to-day, 'noder time him help watch-man.

Man no trabel, him no know puss hab cock-eye (squint).

Man sleep in fowl nest, but fowl nest no him bed.

Man talk plenty, him pay him fader debt.

Maugre (thin) plantain better dan none at all.

Mean man go a' market two time.

Misfortune neber throw cloud.

Monkey no trus' (not to be trusted).

Monkey pickny neber walk on ground.

Mout' say " No," Will say " Yes."

Nanny goat neber scratch him back till him see wall.

Neber call centipede names.

Neber make goat trustee for bread-nut tree.

No catchie, no habie.

No ebry ting you yerry good fe talk.

No fe want of tongue make cow no talk.

No let mudfish tail touch water.

No mind make ship run ashore.

No make one donkey choke you.

No trow away dirty water before you hab clean.

Nyam-nyam (eating) will fill belly, but breeze no fill gut.

Nyam some, leave some tink on to-morrow.

Old fire-stick no hard fe catch.

One daddy fe twenty pickny, but twenty pickny no fe one daddy.

One finger can't catch louse.

One tief no like to see 'noder tief carry long bag.

Packy (a small calabash) neber bear pumpkin.

Parson christen him own pickny first.

Patience make sick man drink water-gruel.

Patience man ride jackass.

Pickny will nyam Ma (his mother), but ma no nyam pickny.

Play wid monkey, no play wi' him tail.
Play wi' puppy, puppy lick you face.
Play-stone kill bird.
Poor pasture make sheep shabby.
Poor neber sorry fe himself.
Puss know him four o'clock (dinner hour).
Put me down softly, me a cracked plate.

Quattie bread (a three-halfpenny loaf) fill monkey belly.

Rain neber fall a' one man door.
Ratta (rat) cunny (cunning), so when puss gone him make
　　merry.
Rockatone (stone) at ribber-bottom (bottom of the river)
　　no know sun hot.

Saftly (softly) saftly catch monkey.
Salt neber say himself sweet.
Sensa (sensible) chicken no cry fe fader, him cry fe food,
　　because, if him hab food, him hab fader.
Seven year no 'nough fe wash speckle off Guinea-hen back.
Sharp spur make maugre horse cut caper.
Shut mout' no catch fly.
Sheep an' goat no all onc.
Sheep hab de worst of food, yet him satisfy.
Shoes alone know if stockings hab hole.
Sickness ride horse come, take foot go away.
Sick man no care fe what doctor care.
Sleep hab no massa.
Spider an' fly can't make bargain.
Stranger no know where de deep water in de pass.
Sweet mout' fly follow coffin go a' hole.
Sweet soup make man drink ants.

Table-napkin want to turn table-cloth.
Talk is de ear food.
Talk some, lef (leave) some.

'Tan (stand) far (off) see better.

"Tank you" no buy half bit bread.

Tiger no 'fraid fe bull-dog.

Time longer dan rope.

To-day fe me, to-morrow fe you.

'Tone (stone) walls hab eyes.

Too much sit down break trowsers.

Tree look eber so sound, woodpecker know what will do fe him.

Trouble in de bush, Annancy bring him in de house.

Trouble neber blow shell (trumpet).

Trouble neber set in like a rain.

Two bull can't 'tan (stand) in one penn.

Two cunning man can't share three bits (a shilling and a penny half-penny).

Water more dan flour.

What man no know is good fe know.

When ashes cold, dog sleep dere.

When belly full, jaw must stop.

When belly full, man break pot.

When black man tief, him tief half a bit (twopence farthing), when buckra tief, him tief whole estate.

When bowl go, packy (a small calabash) come.

When breeze no blow, you no see fowl's back.

When breeze no blow, tree no shake.

When bull ole, him feed a' fence side.

When bull ole, you take hog-meat tee-tie (the trailing stem of a wild convolvulus) fe tie him.

When bull ole, him horn bend.

When bull foot broke, him nyam wi' monkey.

When burying day a' your door, you no pick an' choose gravedigger.

When cloud come, sun no set.

When cockroach make dance, him no ax (invite) fowl.

When cocoa-head meet rich soil, de root bore de ground.

When cotton-tree fall, billy-goat jump over him.

When cow dead, mule laugh.

When cow no hab tail, Goramighty brush fly.

When crab no hab hole, him neber get fat.

When crab walk too much, him lose him claw.

When dog hab too much owner, him sleep widout supper.

When dog maugre, him eye red.

When dog nyam egg, him neber leave off.

When drum done play, Jacky done dance. —

When yie (eye) meet yie, man 'fraid.

When yie (eye) no see, mout' can't talk.

When fire an' water dere, anybody can lib.

When fish come out of sea an' tell you alligator hab fever, believe him. —

When fowl merry, hawk catch him chicken.

When fowl done eat, him wipe him mout' 'pon de ground.

When fowl hab teeth (impossibility).

When fowl drink water him lif' up him head an' say, "Tank God, tank God!" but man drink water an' no say noting (nothing).

When Guinea-fowl cry, him say, Woman no fe play.

When hand full, him hab plenty company.

When hog dead, him no care fe hot water.

When jackass carry salt, him lick de hamper.

When man a magistrate, crooked da follow him.

When man no done grow, him neber should cuss long man.

When man hab raw meat, look fe fire.

When man say him no mind, den him mind.

When man hab plenty, him boil pot.

When man no done climb hill, him should neber trow away him stick.

When man no done cross ribber, him should neber cuss alligator long mout'.

When man dead, grass grow a' him door.

When man drunk, him walk an' 'tagger, woman sit down an' consider.

When man lib well an' grow fat, him walk in pasture an' tell cow "How-dye."

When morass catch fire, land-turtle look for mangrove tree.

N

When pigeon merry, hawk near.

When pot full, pot cover nyam some.

When puss hab money, him buy cheese.

When puss gone out, ratta take him house fe himself.

When puss belly full, him say rat bitter.

When puss dead, ratta take him skin fe make bag.

When ram-goat foot broke, him find him massa door.

When tiger get ole, dog bark after him.

When trouble catch bull-dog, puppy breeches fit him.

When you sleep wi' dog, you catch him flea.

When you trow rockatone (stone) at pig-stye, de pig you
  yerry cry " Quee, quee " is de one you hit.

Words mus' die, but man may lib.

Work is no evil.   It is de yies (eyes) dat are cowards.

Woman rain neber done.

Yellow snake an' fowl no compartner.

You eber see empty bag 'tan' up ?

You eber see puss refuse butter ?

You neber see de day dog nyam dog.

You neber see dog chaw razor.

You neber see empty pot boil over.

You no see mammy, you seek grandy (grandmother).

You shake man han', you no shake him heart.

EDINBURGH : T. AND A. CONSTABLE,
PRINTERS TO THE QUEEN, AND TO THE UNIVERSITY.